Weekend AFGHANS

BY JEAN LEINHAUSER AND RITA WEISS

 STERLING PUBLISHING CO., INC., NEW YORK

We have made every effort to ensure the accuracy and completeness of the instructions in this book.
We cannot, however, be responsible for human error, typographical mistakes or variations in individual work.

Book Design by CBG Graphics, New York, NY
Carol Belanger Grafton, Designer

INTRODUCTION

Hi! Got anything planned for this weekend?

If not, join us on a walk through the pages of this book, and select a beautiful afghan to knit or crochet with big needles and hooks in just a short time.

Our designers have come up with a wide variety of patterns that you can create in limited time for special gifts or for your own enjoyment. There are lacy knits, granny crochet motifs, favorite ripples speeded up to be worked in no time at all.

A special section of baby afghans is sure to be a favorite.

"Weekend" can mean many different things—from the standard Friday-night-to-Monday morning, to a four-day holiday weekend, to a lengthy "lost" weekend when you settle in and really get lost in your work.

Making afghans should, however, be a pleasure. So don't race the clock; take your time and enjoy yourself. If it takes several weeks to make one of our weekend afghans—that's all right with us! There's no prize for the one who finishes first.

We hope this collection of colorful, easy to make afghans brightens up your weekends for months to come.

1455 Linda Vista Dr.
San Marcos, CA 92069

Jean Leinhauser
Rita Weiss

For my parents, Ruth Daggett Leinhauser and Peter Leinhauser, who have always encouraged me in my needlework. J.L.

For my daughter Carla, who needs a little warmth in her life. R.W.

ACKNOWLEDGMENTS

American Thread kindly permitted us to use several designs which we originally created for them in their yarns.

Coats & Clark generously provided several afghan designs, and the color photographs of the finished projects.

Nomis Yarns let us borrow two afghan designs.

Susan Bates generously lent us an afghan especially created for their new size 17 needle.

Special thanks to **Eleanor Denner** whose fingers flew while working above and beyond the call of duty to help us meet our deadline; and to **Carol Mansfield**, who directed all of the beautiful photography that shows off our afghans so well. And we are grateful to **Ann Walas**, **Jack Weiss** and **Carol Mansfield** who let us disrupt their homes to photograph many of the interior shots.

To ensure the accuracy and clarity of our instructions, all of the projects in this book were tested by a group of dedicated and hard-working women, who made the designs which we have photographed. We express our appreciation to the following group of pattern testers:

Tina Anderson, Vista, California
Wendy Dodge, Greeley, Colorado
Carolyn Hawkins, Vista, California
Liz Irvine, Escondido, California
Jean Leinhauser, San Diego, California

Carol Mansfield, San Diego, California
Margaret Miller, Chicago, Illinois
Addie Snett, Northbrook, Illinois
Lee Ann Tibbals, Oceanside, California
Rita Weiss, Escondido, California

CONTENTS

Chapter 6: BABY WEEKENDS   127

INDEX   144

Weekend
AFGHAN
TECHNIQUES

To make your afghaning go more quickly and be more fun, we've included here a complete "refresher course" on the knit and crochet techniques required.

We suggest that you read this section, hook or needles handy, and work through any steps that are unfamiliar to you. There are a number of special techniques that you may not have done before, and be sure to try those.

You certainly don't have to be an expert to make our quick afghans, but you'll enjoy it more if, you're sure of what you're doing.

KNITTING

CASTING ON (CO)

Only one knitting needle is used with this method. First, measure off a length of yarn that allows about 1″ for each stitch you are going to cast on. Make a slip knot on needle as follows. Make a yarn loop, leaving about 4″ length of yarn at free end; insert needle into loop and draw up yarn from free end to make a loop on needle (**Fig 1**). Pull yarn firmly, but not tightly, to form a slip knot on needle (**Fig 2**). This slip knot counts as your first stitch. Now work as follows.

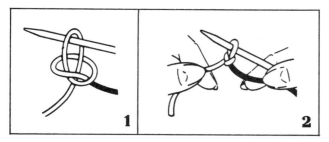

Step 1: Hold needle with slip knot in right hand, with yarn from skein to your right, and measured length of yarn to your left. With left hand, make a yarn loop (**Fig 3**) and insert needle into loop (**Fig 4**).

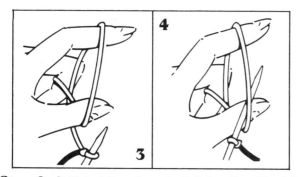

Step 2: Still holding loop in left hand, with right hand, pick up yarn from skein and bring it from back to front around the needle (**Fig 5**).

Step 3: Bring needle through loop and toward you; at the same time, pull gently on yarn end to tighten loop (**Fig 6**). Make it snug but not tight below needle.

You now have one cast-on stitch. Repeat Steps 1 through 3 for each additional stitch desired.

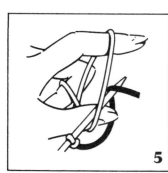

THE KNIT STITCH (K)

Step 1: Hold the needle with cast-on stitches in your left hand. Insert point of right needle in first stitch, from left to right, just as in casting on (**Fig 7**).

Step 2: With right index finger, bring yarn under and over point of right needle (**Fig 8**).

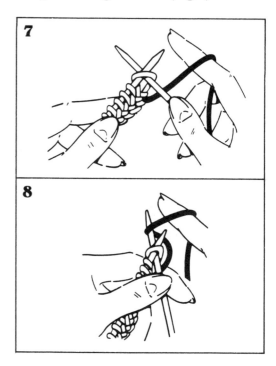

Step 3: Draw yarn through stitch with right needle point (**Fig 9**).

Step 4: Slip the loop on the left needle off, so the new stitch is entirely on the right needle (**Fig 10**).

This completes one knit stitch.

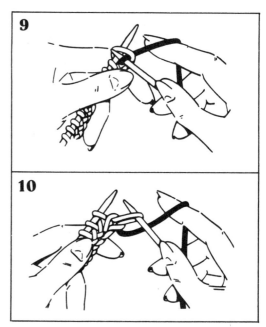

THE PURL STITCH (P)

The reverse of the knit stitch is called the purl stitch. Instead of inserting the right needle point from left to right under the left needle (as you did for the knit stitch), you will now insert it from right to left, in front of the left needle.

Step 1: Insert right needle, from right to left, into first stitch, and in front of left needle (**Fig 11**).

Step 2: Holding yarn in front of work (side toward you), bring it around right needle counterclockwise (**Fig 12**).

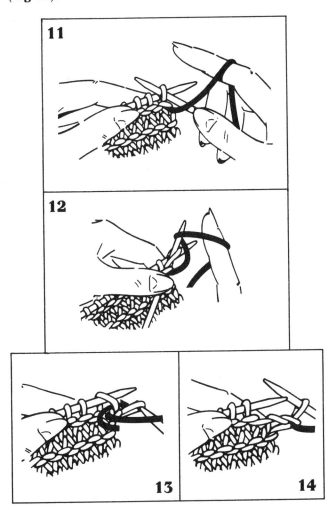

Step 3: With right needle, pull yarn back through stitch (**Fig 13**). Slide stitch off left needle, leaving new stitch on right needle (**Fig 14**).

One purl stitch is now completed.

BINDING OFF (BO)

To bind off on the knit side:
Step 1: Knit the first 2 stitches. Then insert left needle into the first of the 2 stitches (**Fig 15**), and pull it over the second stitch and completely off the needle (**Fig 16**). You have now bound off one stitch.

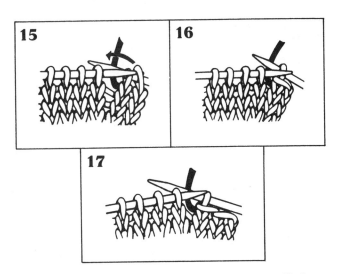

Step 2: Knit one more stitch; insert left needle into first stitch on right needle and pull it over the new stitch and completely off the needle (**Fig 17**). Another stitch is now bound off.

Repeat Step 2 until all sts are bound off and one loop remains on right-hand needle. "Finish off" or "end off" the yarn (cut yarn and draw end through last loop).

To bind off on the purl side:
Step 1: Purl the first 2 stitches. Now insert left needle into the first stitch on right needle, and pull it over the second stitch and completely off the needle. You have now bound off one stitch.

Step 2: Purl one more stitch; insert left needle into first stitch on right needle and pull it over the new stitch and completely off the needle. Another stitch is bound off.

Repeat Step 2 until all sts are bound off.

YARN OVER (YO)

To make a yarn over before a knit stitch, bring yarn to front of work as if you were going to purl, then take it over the right needle to the back into the position for knitting; then knit the next stitch (**Fig 18**).

To make a yarn over before a purl stitch, bring yarn around right needle from front to back, then back around into position for purling; purl the next stitch (**Fig 19**).

INCREASING

Increasing is a shaping technique in which stitches are added, making the knitted piece wider. The most commonly used method to work an increase is to knit (or purl) twice into the same stitch. Another method is called "yarn over," and is used for a decorative increase as in a raglan seam, and for lacy, openwork patterns.

Note
Use this method only when specified in pattern instructions, as it leaves a small hole in your work.

Knit 2 Stitches in One. Step 1: Insert tip of right needle into stitch from front to back as to knit; now knit the stitch in the usual manner but don't remove the stitch from the left needle (**Fig 20**).

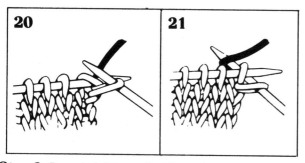

Step 2: Insert right needle (from front to back) into **back** loop of **same** stitch, and knit it again (**Fig 21**), this time slipping the stitch off the left needle. *You have now increased one stitch.*

Purl 2 Stitches in One. Step 1: Insert right needle into stitch from back to front as to purl; now purl the stitch in the usual manner but don't remove the stitch from the left needle.

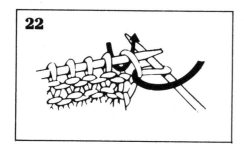

Step 2: Insert right needle (from back to front) into **back** loop of **same** stitch (**Fig 22**) and purl it again, this time slipping the stitch off the left needle. *You have now increased one stitch.*

Yarn Over (between 2 knit stitches): Bring yarn to **front** of work as if you were going to purl, then take it **over** the right needle to **back** of work. Yarn is now in position to knit the next stitch (**Fig 23**). *You have added one stitch.*

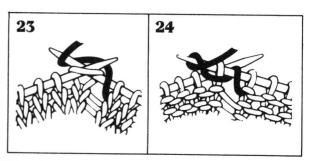

Yarn Over (between 2 purl stitches): Bring yarn **over** right needle to **back** of work, then bring yarn forward between the needles to **front** of work. Yarn is now in position to purl the next stitch (**Fig 24**). *You have added one stitch.*

DECREASING

Another shaping technique is decreasing, in which stitches are taken off, making the knitted piece narrower. These two methods of decreasing are most often used in knitting.

Knit (or purl) 2 Stitches Together: This method, abbreviated K2 tog (P2 tog), is worked simply by knitting (or purling) 2 stitches as one.

To work **K2 tog,** insert right needle through the fronts of first 2 stitches on left needle as to knit (**Fig 25**), then knit these 2 stitches as one (**Fig 26**). *You have decreased one stitch.*

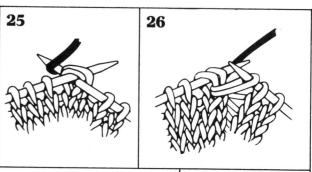

To work **P2 tog,** insert right needle through the fronts of next 2 stitches on left needle as to purl (**Fig 27**), then purl these 2 stitches as one. *You have decreased one stitch.*

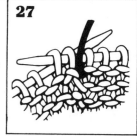

Pass Slipped Stitch Over: This method, abbreviated PSSO, is often used in the shaping of raglans or other pieces where a definite decrease line is desired. To use this method you must first know how to "slip" a stitch, which is an action that transfers a stitch from the left needle to the right needle without working it.

"Slip a stitch as to knit" is used when decreasing. To do this, insert right needle into stitch on left needle as if you were going to knit it; but instead of knitting, slip the stitch from left needle to right needle (**Fig 28**).

"Slip a stitch as to purl" is used when working a pattern stitch, so that on the next row of the pattern, the slipped stitch will be on the needle in the correct position for knitting (or purling). To do this, insert right needle into stitch on left needle as if you were going to purl it; but instead of purling, slip the stitch from left needle to right needle (**Fig 29**).

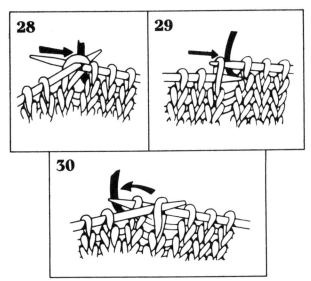

Now that you know how to slip a stitch, you can practice the second method of decreasing.

To work PSSO, slip the next stitch as to knit, then knit the next stitch, now pass the slipped stitch *over* the knitted stitch by using the point of the left needle to lift the slipped stitch over the knitted stitch as in binding off (**Fig 30**).

JOINING YARN

New yarn should be added only at the **beginning** of a row, never in the middle of a row, unless this is required for a color pattern change. To add yarn, tie the new strand around the old strand, making a knot at the edge of work (**Fig 31**), leaving at least a 4″ end on both old and new strands.

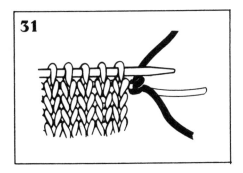

GAUGE AND MEASURING

Gauge simply means the number of stitches per inch, and the number of rows per inch, that result from a specified yarn worked with needles in a specified size. But since everyone knits differently—some loosely, some tightly, some in between—the measurements of individual work will vary greatly, even when the knitters use the exact same pattern and the exact same size yarn and needles.

Needle sizes given in instructions are merely guides, and should never be used without making a 4″ square sample swatch to check your gauge. It is your responsibility to make sure you achieve the gauge specified in the pattern.

To achieve the gauge specified, you may need to use a different needle size—either larger or smaller—than that specified in the pattern. If you have more stitches or rows per inch than specified, you will have to try a size larger needles. If you have fewer stitches or rows per inch than specified, you will have to try a size smaller needles. **Do not hesitate to change to larger or smaller needles if necessary to achieve gauge.**

WEAVING IN ENDS

When you finish your afghan, weave in all the yarn ends securely. To do this, use a size 16 tapestry needle, or a plastic yarn needle, and weave the yarn end through the backs of stitches (**Fig 32**), first weaving about 2″ in one direction and then 1″ in the reverse direction. Cut off excess yarn.

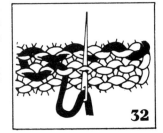

Note
Never weave in more than one yarn end at a time.

CORRECTING MISTAKES

Dropped Stitches: Each time you knit or purl a stitch, take care to pull the stitch off the left needle after completing the new stitch. Otherwise, you will be adding stitches when you don't want to. Don't let a stitch slip off the needle **before** you've knitted or purled it—that's called a **dropped stitch**. Even expert knitters drop a stitch now and then, but it's easy to pick up when you know how. A dropped stitch can be picked up several rows after it has been dropped by using a crochet hook.

To **pick up** a dropped stitch, have the knit side (right side of work) facing you. Insert the crochet hook into the dropped stitch from front to back, under the horizontal strand in the row above (**Fig 33**). Hook the horizontal strand above and pull through the loop on the crochet hook. Continue in this manner up to the working row, then transfer the loop from the crochet hook to the left needle, being careful not to twist it (**Fig 34**).

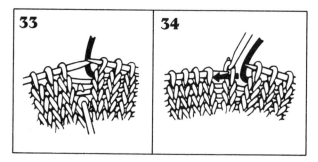

Unraveling Stitches: Sometimes it is necessary to unravel a large number of stitches, even down several rows, to correct a mistake. Whenever possible, carefully unravel the stitches one-by-one by putting the needle into the row below (**Fig 35**) and undoing the stitch above, until the mistake is reached.

If several rows need to be unraveled, carefully slide all stitches off the needle and unravel each row down to the row in which the error occurred. Then unravel this row, stitch by stitch, placing each stitch back on the needle in the correct position, without twisting it.

FOR LEFT HANDERS...

Many left-handed people learn to knit by reversing the stitches—a method we do not recommend. Instead, we suggest lefties try the Continental Method, in which the left hand does more of the work than the right.

Here is how to work in the Continental Method:

Knitting: Hold yarn in left hand, over index finger, as in **Fig 36**.

Step 1: Insert point of right needle into front of stitch on left needle as to knit.

Step 2: Catch yarn with point of right needle and draw yarn through (**Fig 37**), making a new loop.

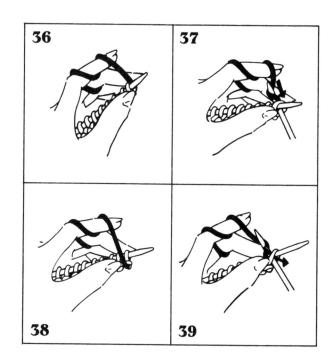

Step 3: Slip stitch off left needle: one knit stitch made. Repeat Steps 1 through 3 across row.

Purling: Hold yarn in left hand, over index finger, in front of work (**Fig 38**).

Step 1: Insert point of right needle into front of stitch on left needle as to purl, keeping it behind yarn on left index finger.

Step 2: Catch yarn around point of right needle (**Fig 39**) and draw yarn backward and up through stitch, making a new loop.

Step 3: Slip stitch off left needle: one purl stitch made. Repeat Steps 1 through 3 across row.

CROCHETING

CHAIN (ch)

Crochet always starts with a basic chain. To begin, make a slip loop on hook (**Fig 40**), leaving a 4″ tail of yarn.

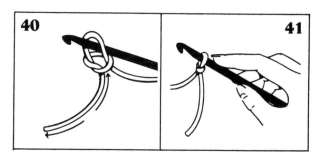

Step 1: Take a hook in right hand, holding it between thumb and third finger (**Fig 41**), and rest index finger near tip of hook.

Step 2: Take slip loop in thumb and index finger of left hand (**Fig 42**) and bring yarn over third finger of left hand, catching it loosely at left palm with remaining two fingers.

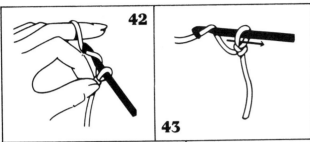

Step 3: Bring yarn over hook from back to front (**Fig 43**), and draw through loop on hook.

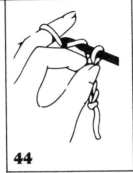

One chain made. Repeat Step 3 for each additional chain desired, moving your left thumb and index finger up close to the hook after each stitch or two (**Fig 44**).

When counting number of chains, do not count the loop on the hook or the starting slip knot.

SINGLE CROCHET (sc)

First, make a chain to desired length.

Step 1: Insert hook in top loop of 2nd chain from hook (**Fig 45**); hook yarn (bring yarn over hook from back to front) and draw through (**Fig 46**).

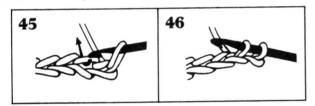

Step 2: Hook yarn and draw through 2 loops on hook (**Fig 47**).

One single crochet made. Work a single crochet (repeat Steps 1 and 2) in each remaining chain.

To work additional rows, chain 1 and turn work counterclockwise. Inserting hook under 2 top loops of the stitch (**Fig 48**), work a single crochet (as before) in each stitch across.

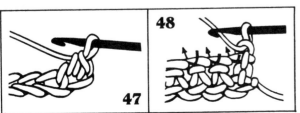

DOUBLE CROCHET (dc)

Double crochet is a taller stitch than single crochet. Begin by making a chain to desired length.

Step 1: Bring yarn once over the hook; insert hook in the top loop of the 4th chain from hook (**Fig 49**). Hook yarn and draw through (**Fig 50**).

Step 2: Hook yarn and draw through first 2 loops on hook (**Fig 51**).

Step 3: Hook yarn and draw through last 2 loops on hook (**Fig 52**).

One double crochet made. Work a double crochet (repeat Steps 1 through 3) in each remaining chain.

To work additional rows, make 3 chains and turn work counterclockwise. Beginning in 2nd stitch (**Fig 53**—3 chains count as first double crochet), work a double crochet (as before) in each stitch across (remember to insert hook under 2 top loops of stitch). At end of row, work last double crochet in the top chain of chain-3 (**Fig 54**).

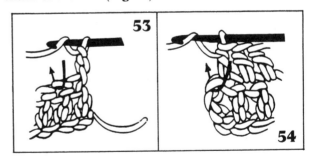

HALF DOUBLE CROCHET (hdc)

This stitch eliminates one step of double crochet—hence its name. It is taller than single crochet, but shorter than double crochet. Begin by making a chain to desired length.

Step 1: Bring yarn over hook; insert hook in top loop of 3rd chain from hook, hook yarn and draw through (3 loops now on hook).

Step 2: Hook yarn and draw through all 3 loops on hook (**Fig 55**).

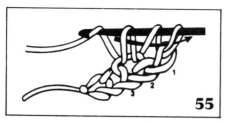

55

One half double crochet made. Work a half double crochet (repeat Steps 1 and 2) in each remaining chain.

To work additional rows, make 2 chains and turn work counterclockwise. Beginning in 2nd stitch (2 chains count as first half double crochet), work a half double crochet (as before) in each stitch across. At end of row, work last half double crochet in the top chain of chain-2.

TRIPLE CROCHET (tr)

Triple crochet is a tall stitch that works up quickly. First, make a chain to desired length.

Step 1: Bring yarn twice over the hook, insert hook in 5th chain from hook (**Fig 56**); hook yarn and draw through (**Fig 57**).

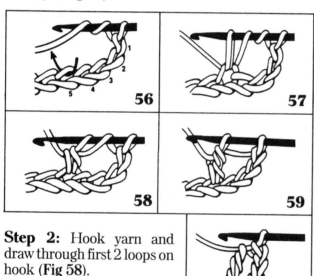

56

57

58

59

Step 2: Hook yarn and draw through first 2 loops on hook (**Fig 58**).

Step 3: Hook yarn and draw through next 2 loops on hook (**Fig 59**).

60

Step 4: Hook yarn and draw through remaining 2 loops on hook (**Fig 60**).

One triple crochet made. Work a triple crochet (repeat Steps 1 through 4) in each remaining chain.

To work additional rows, make 4 chains and turn work counterclockwise. Beginning in 2nd stitch (4 chains count as first triple crochet), work a double crochet (as before) in each stitch across. At end of row, work last triple crochet in the top chain of chain-4.

SLIP STITCH (sl st)

This is the shortest of all crochet stitches, and usually is used to join work, or to move yarn across a group of stitches without adding height. To practice, make a chain to desired length; then work one row of double crochets.

Step 1: Insert hook in first st; hook yarn and draw through both stitch and loop on hook in one motion (**Fig 61**).

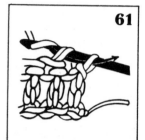

61

One slip stitch made. Work a slip stitch (repeat Step 1) in each stitch across.

INCREASING AND DECREASING

Shaping is usually accomplished either by increasing, which adds stitches to make the crocheted piece wider; or decreasing, which subtracts stitches to make the piece narrower.

Increasing: To increase one stitch—in single, half double, double or triple crochet, simply work two stitches in one stitch.

Decreasing: A simple method of decreasing is to skip a stitch, but this is usually undesirable, as it will leave a hole in your work. The preferred way is to work two stitches into one stitch. Practice each technique on a sample swatch of the stitch used in the decrease method.

Decreasing in Single Crochet: Draw up a loop in each of the next 2 stitches (3 loops now on hook), hook yarn and draw through all 3 loops on hook (**Fig 62**). Single crochet decrease made (**Fig 63**).

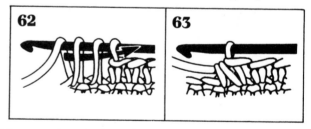

62

63

Decreasing in Double Crochet: Work a double crochet in the first stitch until 2 loops remain on hook (**Fig 64**). Keeping these 2 loops on hook, work another double crochet in the next (2nd) stitch until 3 loops remain on hook, hook yarn and draw through all 3 loops on hook (**Fig 65**). Double crochet decrease made (**Fig 66**).

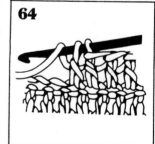

64

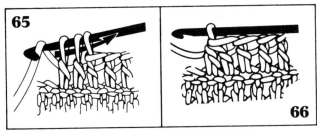

Decreasing in Half Double Crochet: Work a half double crochet in the first stitch until 3 loops remain on hook (**Fig 67**). Keeping these 3 loops on hook, draw up a loop in the next (2nd) stitch (4 loops now on hook), hook yarn and draw through all 4 loops on hook (**Fig 68**). Half double crochet decrease made (**Fig 69**).

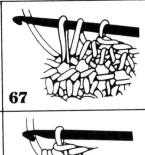

Decreasing in Triple Crochet: Work a triple crochet in the first stitch until 2 loops remain on hook (**Fig 70**). Keeping these 2 loops on hook, work another triple crochet in the next (2nd) stitch until 3 loops remain on hook, hook yarn and draw through all 3 loops on hook (**Fig 71**). Triple crochet decrease made (**Fig 72**).

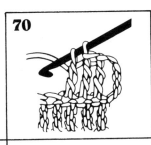

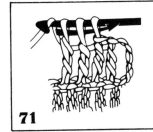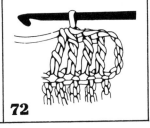

JOINING NEW YARN

Never tie or leave knots! In crochet, yarn ends can be easily worked in and hidden because of the density of the stitches. Always leave at least 4″ ends when finishing off yarn just used and joining new yarn. If a flaw or knot appears in the yarn while you are working from a ball or skein, cut out the imperfection and rejoin the yarn.

Whenever possible, join new yarn at the end of a row. To do this, work the last stitch with the old yarn until 2 loops remain on hook, then with new yarn complete the stitch (**Fig 73**).

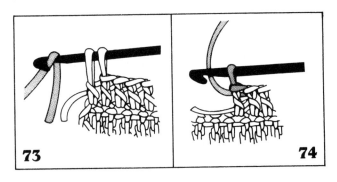

To join new yarn in the middle of a row, when about 12″ of the old yarn remains, work several more stitches with the old yarn, working the stitches over the end of new yarn. Then change yarns in stitch as previously explained (**Fig 74**). Continuing with new yarn, work the following stitches over the old yarn end.

GAUGE

This is the most important aspect of crochet—if you don't work to gauge, your crocheted projects will never be the correct size, and you may not have enough yarn to finish your project.

Gauge means the number of stitches per inch, and rows per inch, that result from a specified yarn worked with a specified size hook. But since everyone crochets differently—some loosely, some tightly, some in between—the measurements of individual work can vary greatly when using the same size hook and yarn. It is your responsibility to make sure you achieve the gauge specified in the pattern.

Hook sizes given in instructions are merely guides and should never be used without making a 4″ square sample swatch to check gauge. Do not hesitate to change to a larger or smaller size hook if necessary to achieve gauge. If you get more stitches per inch than specified, try again with a larger size hook. If you get fewer stitches per inch than specified, try again with a smaller size hook. Keep trying until you find the size hook that will give you the specified gauge.

If you have the correct number of stitches per inch, but cannot achieve the row gauge, adjust the height of your stitches. This means that after inserting the hook to begin a new stitch, draw up a little more yarn if your stitches are not tall enough—this makes the first loop slightly higher; or draw up less yarn if your stitches are too tall. Practice will help you achieve the correct height.

FRINGE

BASIC INSTRUCTIONS

Cut a piece of cardboard about 6″ wide and half as long as specified in instructions for strands plus ½″ for trimming allowance. Wind yarn loosely and evenly lengthwise around cardboard. When card is filled, cut yarn across one end. Do this several times, then begin fringing; you can wind additional strands as you need them.

SINGLE KNOT FRINGE

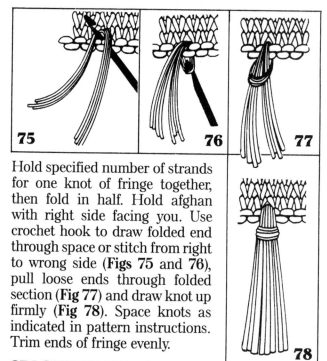

Hold specified number of strands for one knot of fringe together, then fold in half. Hold afghan with right side facing you. Use crochet hook to draw folded end through space or stitch from right to wrong side (**Figs 75** and **76**), pull loose ends through folded section (**Fig 77**) and draw knot up firmly (**Fig 78**). Space knots as indicated in pattern instructions. Trim ends of fringe evenly.

SPAGHETTI FRINGE

Each knot is tied with just one strand of yarn. Use same knotting method as for Single Knot Fringe.

DOUBLE KNOT FRINGE

Begin by working Single Knot Fringe completely across one end of afghan. With right side facing you and working from left to right, take half the strands of one knot and half the strands in the knot next to it, and knot them together (**Fig 79**).

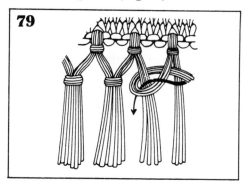

TRIPLE KNOT FRINGE

First work Double Knot Fringe. Then working again on right side from left to right, tie third row of knots as in **Fig 80**.

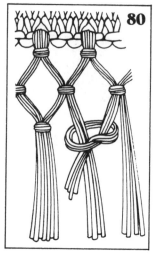

BASIC GRANNY SQUARE

This pattern lets you practice the basic techniques of granny squares, but when making a specific project in this book or any other source, follow the *exact* instructions given, as there are slight differences in working methods of different motifs.

Make a sl knot on hook with first color, leaving a 3″ end. Ch 4, join with a sl st to form a ring (**Fig 81**).

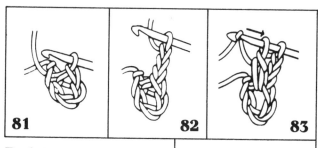

Rnd 1: [On this round, you will be working *into* the ring. As you do this, also work over the 3″ end left after making the sl knot; this keeps down the number of yarn ends to be run in after the square is completed.] Ch 3 (**Fig 82**), 2 dc in ring (**Fig 83** shows first dc being worked in ring); (ch 2, 3 dc in ring) 3 times; ch 2, join in 3rd ch of beg ch-3 with a sl st (**Fig 84**). [The side of the work now facing you is called the *right side* of the work.] Finish off first color.

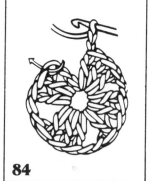

Rnd 2: Make a sl knot on hook with 2nd color; with right side of work facing you, join 2nd color with a sl st in any ch-2 sp (these are corner sps); ch 3, 2 dc in same sp (**Fig 85** shows first dc being worked in sp); ch 2, 3 dc again in same sp; * in next ch-2 sp, work (3 dc, ch 2, 3 dc); rep from * twice, join with a sl st in

3rd ch of beg ch-3. Finish off 2nd color. Look at your work; you should now have a perfect square.

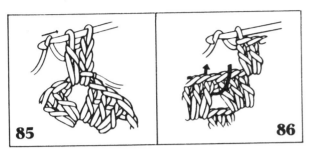

Rnd 3: With right side of work facing you, join 3rd color as before in any ch-2 corner sp; (ch 3, 2 dc, ch 2, 3 dc) all in same sp; between next two 3-dc groups (**Fig 86**), work 3 dc for side; * (3 dc, ch 2, 3 dc) all in next ch-2 sp for corner; 3 dc between next two 3-dc groups for side; rep from * twice, join with a sl st in 3rd ch of beg ch-3. Finish off 3rd color.

Rnd 4: With right side of work facing you, join 4th color as before in any ch-2 corner sp; (ch 3, 2 dc, ch 2, 3 dc) all in same sp; * (3 dc between next two 3-dc groups) twice for side; (3 dc, ch 2, 3 dc) all in next ch-2 sp for corner; rep from * twice; (3 dc between next two 3-dc groups) twice for side; join with a sl st in 3rd ch of beg ch-3. Finish off 4th color. Weave in all loose yarn ends; trim them off.

Notes

1. You now have a 4-rnd square; work any additional desired rnds as for Rnd 4, working one more side group of 3 dcs on every additional rnd.

2. Unless a pattern specifies that you must *turn* your work before each new rnd, always work with the right side facing you.

3. When a pattern calls for working 2 or more rnds of the same color in succession, work to end of rnd, join, but do not finish off. Sl st in tops of each of next 2 dcs and into corner sp; work next rnd as specified.

4. When making grannys, you'll have lots of yarn ends to weave in (do this securely). Make it a practice to weave these in as you finish each square, unless the pattern says not to.

JOINING

When joining granny squares or other pieces of crochet, we often tell you to sew through back loops only. Do this with an overcast stitch, working through the outer loops as shown in **Fig 87**. Take care not to pull the sewing stitches too tightly.

EDGINGS

Single Crochet Edging: Upon completion of a project, it is sometimes necessary to finish an edge. The instructions will say to "work a row of single crochet, taking care to keep work flat." This means to adjust your stitches as you work. You may need to skip a row or stitch here or there to keep the edging from rippling; or add a stitch to keep the work from pulling in. When working around a corner, it is usually necessary to work 3 stitches in the center corner stitch to keep the corner flat and square.

Reverse Single Crochet Edging: This edging produces a lovely corded effect and is usually worked after a row of single crochet. It is worked on the right side **from left to right** (the opposite direction for working single crochet). Work one reverse single crochet in each stitch across (see **Figs 88 and 89**).

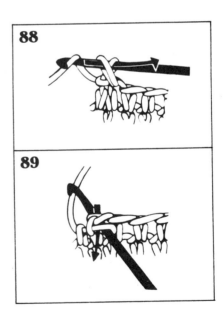

SYMBOLS

*An asterisk is used to mark the beginning of a portion of instructions which will be worked more than once; thus, "rep from * twice" means after working the instructions once, repeat the instructions following the asterisk twice more (3 times in all).

†The dagger identifies a portion of instructions that will be repeated again later in the pattern.

:The number after a colon at the end of a row indicates the number of stitches you should have when the row has been completed.

( )Parentheses are used to enclose instructions which should be worked the exact number of times specified immediately following the parentheses, such as (K1, P1) twice. They are also used to set off and clarify a group of sts that are to be worked all into the same sp or st, such as (2 dc, ch 1, 2 dc) in corner sp.

[ ]Brackets and ( ) parentheses are used to provide additional information to clarify instructions.

ABBREVIATIONS

KNIT ABBREVIATIONS

BO	bind off
CO	cast on
dpn	double pointed needle
K	knit
P	purl
PSSO	pass slipped stitch over
stock st	stockinette stitch (knit 1 row, purl 1 row)

CROCHET ABBREVIATIONS

ch(s)	chain(s)
dc	double crochet(s)
hdc	half double crochet(s)
sc	single crochet(s)
sl st(s)	slip stitch(es)
Tch	turning chain
trc	triple crochet(s)

KNIT AND CROCHET ABBREVIATIONS

beg	begin(ning)	prev	previous	sl	slip
dec	decrease (-ing)	rem	remain(ing)	sp(s)	space(s)
Fig	figure	rep	repeat(ing)	st(s)	stitch(es)
inc	increase (-ing)	rnd(s)	round(s)	tog	together
patt	pattern	sk	skip	YO	yarn over

WORK EVEN   This term in instructions means to continue working in the pattern as established, without increasing or decreasing.

18

CHAPTER 2

VERY SHORT
Weekends

These are our very quickest to make afghans—you can probably turn one out in two nights and a day—created for those times when time is at a premium, but you still want to finish a beautiful project. Two of these quickies are in a small size we call Lapghans—ideal for covering the knees. Another quickie is already fringed when you've completed work.

[CROCHETED]

Pumpkin Shell

designed by Eleanor Denner

Take a pretty shell pattern; work it in bright orange yarn—and you've got a Pumpkin Shell! This quick and easy afghan would be pretty in any color.

Size

36″ × 55″

Materials

Worsted weight yarn:
    28 oz orange
Size K aluminum crochet hook *(or size required for gauge)*

Gauge

Shell of (3 trc, ch 3, 3 trc) = 2½″

Instructions

Ch 115.

Row 1: Sc in 2nd ch from hook and in each ch across; ch 4, turn.

Row 2: Sk 4 sc * shell of (3 trc, ch 3, 3 trc) all in next sc; sk 6 sc; rep from * across, trc in last sc, ch 4, turn.

Row 3: * Shell of (3 trc, ch 3, 3 trc) all in ch-3 sp; rep from * across, trc in top of turning ch; ch 4, turn.

Rep Row 3 until piece measures 55″. At end of last row, ch 9, turn.

Next Row: * Sc in ch-3 sp, ch 6; rep from * to last ch-3 sp, ch 4, trc in top of turning ch, ch 1, turn.

Last Row: Sc in first st, 3 sc in next sp; * sc in next sc, 6 sc in ch-6 sp; rep from * to last sp, 3 sc in last sp, sc in top of turning ch, finish off.

FRINGE

Work Single Knot Fringe (see page 16) across each short end. Cut strands 16″ long; use 8 strands in each knot, and tie a knot in every other stitch.

[KNITTED]

Angel Lace

designed by Eleanor Denner

Light, lacy, fit for an angel! That's this pretty and extra easy afghan, knitted in bright white. Try it in a pastel color, too.

Size

54″ × 75″ before fringing

Materials

Worsted weight yarn:
    20 oz white
Size 17 circular knitting needle *(or size required for gauge)*

Gauge

3 sts = 2″

Instructions

Cast on 131 sts. Do not join. Work back and forth in rows

Row 1: * K1, YO; rep from * across, ending K1.

Row 2: * K1, drop YO of previous row; rep from * across ending K1.

Rep Rows 1 and 2 until piece measures 54″. Bind off very loosely.

FRINGE

Place Single Knot Fringe (see page 16) across each long end. Cut strands 20″ long and use 2 strands in each knot. Place knot in every other stitch across.

[CROCHETED]

Café au Lait

designed by Eleanor Denner

This airy afghan looks light and breezy, but traps the air like a thermal blanket to keep the user toasty warm.

Size

42″ × 54″ before fringing

Materials

Worsted weight yarn:
  16 oz beige
Size K aluminum crochet hook *(or size required for gauge)*

Gauge

3 trc = 1″

Instructions

Ch 112.

Row 1: Trc in 4th ch from hook and in each ch across; ch 3, turn.

Row 2: Skip first trc, trc in next 2 sts; * ch 1, skip 1 trc, trc in next trc; rep from * to last 3 trc and turning ch, ch 1, sk 1 trc, trc in next 2 sts and in top of turning ch, ch 3, turn.

Row 3: Skip first trc, trc in next 2 trc and in ch-1 sp; * ch 1, sk next trc, trc in ch-1 sp; rep from * across, ending trc in last 2 sts and in turning ch; ch 3, turn.

Row 4: Skip first trc, trc in next 2 sts; * ch 1, skip next trc, trc in next ch-1 sp; rep from * across, ending ch 1, skip 1 trc, trc in next 2 trc, trc in turning ch; ch 3, turn.

Rep rows 3 and 4 until piece measures approx 60″.

Last Row: Trc in each trc and in each ch-1 sp across. Finish off.

EDGING

Work one row of sc around entire afghan, adjusting stitches to keep work flat. Then work one row reverse single crochet around. Finish off.

[CROCHETED]
No Sew Granny

This beautiful combination of colors creates a striking Granny Lapghan—sized just right to throw over your knees. This size makes a super gift for someone in a wheelchair.

Size

31″ × 41″

Materials

Nomis Lustro worsted weight yarn (100 gr. skeins)
- 4 white *(Color A)*
- 1 aqua *(Color B)*
- 1 apricot *(Color C)*
- 1 yellow *(Color D)*

Size I aluminum crochet hook *(or size required for gauge)*

Gauge

3 rnd granny sq = 3″

Instructions

SQUARE 1 (make 12)

With Color B ch 5, join to beg ch with sl st to form a ring.

Rnd 1: Ch 4 (counts as dc, ch 1) [3 dc in ring, ch 1] 3 times, 2 dc in ring. Join this and every rnd to 3rd ch of beg ch 4 with sl st, cut yarn leaving a 1 inch end. With crochet hook work end in outer edge of completed rnd in following manner: * insert hook through back loop of next st, hook and draw end through. Repeat from * until end is worked in.

Rnd 2: Right side facing (right side is rnd just completed), this and every rnd, join Color C in any ch-sp leaving a 1 inch end, ch 4, turn. Lay a 1 inch end over finished edge of previous rnd, 2 dc in same sp and over 1 inch end. Work 3rd dc in same sp drawing remaining end into st [3 dc, ch 1, 3 dc all in next ch-sp] 3 times, 2 dc in beg sp. Join.

Rnd 3: Repeat joining procedure of rnd 2 on this and every rnd. Join Color D in any ch-sp, ch 4, turn, 3 dc in same sp, [3 dc in next sp (between 3 dc groups of previous rnd), 3 dc, ch 1, 3 dc all in ch-sp] 3 times, 3 dc in next sp, 2 dc in beg sp. Join.

SQUARE 2 (make 12)

Work same as Square 1, reversing color sequence, using Colors D, C and B.

PANELS (make 5)

Square 1/Rnd 4: Join Color A. Repeat rnd 3 working two 3 dc groups each side of sq. Join.

Square 2/Rnd 4: Joining rnd: repeat rnd 3 working two 3 dc groups each side to 2nd corner, * 3 dc in ch-sp, pick up and hold completed sq 1 in back of sq 2 with wrong sides facing, sc in corner ch-sp of sq 1, return to sq 2, 3 dc in same corner sp, [sc in next sp of sq 1, return to sq 2, 3 dc in next sp] 3 times, sc in corner ch-sp of sq 1, return to sq 2, 3 dc in same corner sp. Squares joined. Complete sq 2 to end. Continue joining in this manner rotating sq 1 and 2 until 8 sq are joined.

EDGING

With right sides facing you, join Color A in upper left corner ch-sp.

Rnd 1: Ch 4, turn, 3 dc in same sp, ** 3 dc in each sp to corner, 3 dc, ch 1, 3 dc turning corner, 3 dc in each of next 3 sp * skip corner ch-sp, 3 dc in joining sp between 2 sq, next sq: skip corner ch-sp, 3 dc in each of next 3 sp * **. Repeat between *'s to lower left corner, 3 dc, ch 1, 3 dc turning corner. Repeat between **'s to end, 2 dc in beg sp. Join.

Rnd 2: Join Color D in any corner, ch 4, turn, 3 dc in same sp, 3 dc in each sp, 3 dc, ch 1, 3 dc turning corners around end, 2 dc in beg sp. Join.

Rnds 3, 4 and 5: Repeat rnd 2 of edging using Colors C, B and A.

JOINING PANELS

Panel 1/Rnd 6: With right side facing sq 1 and end of panel join Color A in upper left corner, repeat rnd 2 of edging to end.

Panel 2/Rnd 6: With right side facing sq 2 at end of panel join Color A in upper left corner, repeat panel 1 to corner. Repeat from * of sq 2. Joining rnd 4: Holding completed panel 1 in back of panel 2, wrong sides facing to lower left corner, complete panel 2 to end.

Panel 3: Repeat panel 2 joining, rnd 6, rotating sq 1 and 2 at end of the panel.

OUTER EDGING

Rnd 1: Using Color A to end: Repeat Panel edging rnd 1 working 3 dc in joining st between panels to end.

Rnd 2: Ch 4, turn, 3 dc in same sp, 3 dc in each sp, 3 dc, ch 1, 3 dc, turning corners to end. Finish off, weave in all ends.

28

[CROCHETED]

Peppermint Stripes

designed by Eleanor Denner

This cheerful afghan features the popular ripple motif, worked in triple crochet. Two colors and white are combined for a refreshing look.

Size

30″ × 45″ before fringing

Materials

Worsted weight yarn:
    12 oz white
    8 oz pink
    8 oz mint
Size K aluminum crochet hook *(or size required for gauge)*

Gauge

One strip = 6″ wide

Instructions

STRIP (make 2 pink, 2 white, 1 green)

Ch 21 loosely.

Row 1: Trc in 5th ch from hook; sk next ch, trc in next 6 chs, 3 trc in next ch; trc in next 6 chs, sk 1 ch, trc in last ch; ch 3, turn.

Row 2: *(Ch 3 counts as first trc of row)* Sk next trc, (trc in next st, ch 1, sk 1) 3 times; sk next trc, (trc, ch 1, trc) all in next st; (ch 1, sk next st, trc in next st) 3 times; ch 1, sk 2 trc, trc in top of turning ch; ch 3, turn.

Row 3: Trc in first ch-1 sp, trc in each st and in each ch-1 sp to center sp; 3 trc in center sp, trc in each st and in each ch-1 sp across, trc in top of turning ch.

Rep rows 2 and 3 until piece measures 45″ long, ending by working row 3. Finish off.

Note

Be sure all strips have the same number of rows.

FINISHING

Sew strips together with overcast st, with right sides facing. Place pink strip in center, with a white strip on each side. Use mint strips at each outside edge.

FRINGE

Cut strands of each color 10″ long. Use 4 strands in each knot and work Single Knot Fringe (see page 16) along each short end, matching fringe color to strip color.

[CROCHETED]

Self Fringing Afghan
designed by Eleanor Denner

This unusual afghan creates its own fringe along the sides as you work! It's made with two strands of yarn in an easy hdc/ch pattern.

Size

40″ × 58″

Materials

Worsted weight yarn:
    24 oz white
    24 oz slate blue
Size K aluminum crochet hook *(or size required for gauge)*

Gauge

In patt, 5 groups of hdc + 3 chs = 5½″

Notes

1. Afghan is worked with 2 strands of yarn throughout.

2. To create side fringe, leave a 6″ strand of yarn free at beg and end of each row. Each new row starts with new yarn.

Instructions

With blue (remember to leave 6″ of yarn at beg and end of row), ch 133. Finish off yarn.

Row 1: Join white; hdc in first ch; * ch 3, sk 3 chs, hdc in next ch; rep from * across, ending with an hdc; finish off yarn, turn work.

Row 2: Join blue; hdc in first hdc; * ch 3, hdc in next hdc; rep from * across, finish off yarn, turn work.

Alternating colors, rep Row 2 until afghan measures 58″ long.

[CROCHETED]
Puff Stitch Afghan

An unusual Granny square accents this charming Lapghan, made in our favorite size. It's perfect to warm your knees as you watch TV, travel in the back seat of a car, or curl up for a nap.

Size

30″ × 43″ before fringing

Materials

Nomis Lustro worsted weight yarn (100 gr skeins)
    6 aqua
Size H crochet hook *(or size required for gauge)*

Gauge

Square = 7″

Instructions

SQUARE (make 24)

Working with 2 strands of yarn held together, ch 5; join with sl st in beg ch to form a ring.

Rnd 1: Ch 1, 7 sc in ring, join to beg ch with sl st (join every rnd with sl st to specified st).

Rnd 2: Draw remaining loop on hook up 1½″ * [YO hook, insert hook in same sp, YO and draw up loop 1½″] 5 times (11 loops on hook), YO and draw through all loops on hook, ch 1 firmly (closing ch = cc) puff st (ps) made, ch 2 *. Repeat between *'s 7 times more (8ps); join to cc.

Rnd 3: Ch 1, sc in same sp, 2 sc in ch 2 sp, [sc in cc, 2 sc in ch 2 sp] 7 times; join to beg ch (24 sc).

Rnd 4: Draw remaining loop on hook up 1½″ [ps, ch 2, ps all in same sp, dc in each of next 5 sts] 4 times; join to cc.

Rnd 5: Sl st this and every rnd into ch-sp, ch 3, 2 sc in same sp, [* sc in cc, sc in each of next 5 dc, sc in cc*, (2 sc, ch 2, 2 sc) all in ch 2 sp] 3 times. Repeat between *'s once, end sc in beg sp; join to first ch of beg ch 3.

Rnd 6: Ch 6, turn, dc in same sp, ch 1, * [skip first st, dc in next st, ch 1] 5 times, (dc, ch 3, dc) all in ch 2 sp, ch 1 *. Repeat between *'s 2 times more. Repeat from [to] 5 times; join to 3rd ch of beg ch 6.

Rnd 7: Ch 3, turn, 2 sc in same sp, sc in dc * [sc in ch-sp, sc in dc] 6 times, (2 sc, ch 2, 2 sc) all in ch 3 sp, sc in dc *. Repeat between *'s 2 times more. Repeat from [to] 6 times, sc in beg sp; join to first ch of beg ch (17 sc, ch 2 each side).

Rnd 8: Ch 6, turn, dc in same sp, * [dc in each of next 17 sts *, (dc, ch 3, dc) all in ch 2 sp] 3 times. Repeat between *'s once; join to 3rd ch of beg ch 6. (19 dc, ch 3 each side).

Rnd 9: Ch 3, turn, sc in same sp, * [sc in each of next 19 sts *, (sc, ch 2, sc) all in ch 2 sp] 3 times. Repeat between *'s once; join to first ch of beg ch 3 (21 sc, ch 2 each side). Finish off.

FINISHING

With right sides facing, sew squares together with overcast st, working in outer lps only and carefully matching sts. Sew 4 squares across, 6 squares long.

EDGING

Hold afghan with right side facing you. Join yarn in any outer corner ch-3 sp, (sc, ch 2, sc) all in same sp; sc in next st, * ch 3, sl st into first ch (picot made); sc in each of next 3 sts; rep from * around, working (sc, ch 2, sc) in each outer corner sp. At end, join with a sl st to beg sc, finish off. Weave in all ends. Lightly steam on wrong side.

[CROCHETED]

Super Quick Ripple

designed by Eleanor Denner

This design can be finished in a jiffy! If you hear about a cold snap in the morning, you can probably have it made to cuddle under by evening. Two strands of yarn in different colors are used, which lets you experiment with many pretty combinations. Try navy with red, gold with brown, or light and dark pink for a feminine look.

Size

62″ × 62″ before fringing

Materials

Worsted weight yarn:
    20 oz green
    20 oz white
Size Q plastic crochet hook *(or size required for gauge)*

Gauge

In pattern, 4 trc = 4″

> ### Note
> Work with 1 strand of green and 1 strand of white held together throughout.

Instructions

Ch 25.

Row 1: Trc in 4th ch from hook and in next 3 chs; sk 2 chs, trc in next 5 chs; 5 trc all in next ch; trc in next 5 chs, sk 2 chs, trc in last 4 chs, ch 3, turn.

Row 2: Sk first trc, trc in next 3 trc, sk 2 trc, trc in next 5 trc, 5 trc all in next trc; trc in each of next 5 trc, sk 2 trc, trc in last 4 trc, ch 3, turn.

Rep Row 2 until piece measures 62″. Finish off, weave in all ends. This completes one strip. Make two more strips, taking care that all three have the same number of rows.

ASSEMBLY

Hold two strips with right sides facing, and sew together with overcast stitch, carefully matching rows. Join third strip in same manner.

FRINGE

Follow Single Knot Fringe Instructions on page 16. Work Single Knot Fringe across each short end. Cut strands 16″ long and use 4 strands (two of each color) in each knot. Space knots in every stitch across.

[CROCHETED]

Pralines 'n Cream

designed by Eleanor Denner

This lovely lacy afghan looks just like our favorite ice cream flavor. Use it to warm up after a triple dip cone!

Size

45″ × 60″

Materials

Worsted weight yarn:
    16 oz white
    24 oz lt tan
Size Q plastic crochet hook

Note

Afghan is worked with 1 strand of tan and 1 strand of white used together throughout.

Special Technique

A Puff St is used throughout this pattern. To make it, work as follows:

YO hook, insert hook in next st and draw up a lp, YO and through 2 lps on hook; YO, insert hook again in same st, draw up a lp, YO and through 2 lps, YO and draw through all 3 sps on hook: Puff St made.

Instructions

Ch 53.

Row 1: Sc in 2nd ch from hook and in each ch across: 52 sc; ch 3, turn.

Row 2: Sk 1 sc, * (trc, ch 1, trc) all in next sc; sk 2 sc, (Puff St, ch 2, Puff St) all in next st; sk 2 sc; rep from * across, trc in last sc, ch 4, turn.

Row 3: Work (trc, ch 1, trc) in each ch-1 sp and work (Puff St, ch 2, Puff St) in each ch-2 sp across row, trc in top of turning ch, ch 4, turn.

Rep Row 3 until piece measures approx 60″; ch 1, turn.

Last Row: Sc in each trc, each Puff St and each ch sp. Finish off, weave in all ends.

FRINGE

Work Single Knot Fringe (see page 16) along each short end, using tan yarn only. Cut strands 16″ long and use 5 strands in each knot.

CHAPTER 3

DATELESS
Weekends

These afghans are ideal for the ordinary weekend—three evenings and two days—when there's nothing exciting on your schedule. Maybe there's a blizzard on its way; or it's 102 degrees outside and you want to stay inside with the air conditioning. Whatever the reason, these varied afghans will keep you busy.

[CROCHETED]

Midshipman

designed by Eleanor Denner

Bright blue and white give a nautical look to this quick afghan which is a nice, light weight.

Size

52″ × 60″ before fringing

Materials

Worsted weight yarn:
>   12 oz white
>   24 oz blue

Size K aluminum crochet hook *(or size required for gauge)*

Gauge

3 dc = 1″

Instructions

With blue, loosely ch 118.

Row 1: Dc in 4th ch from hook and in each ch across; ch 4, turn.

Row 2: Work 3 trc in 4th dc, sk 2 dc; * 3 trc in next dc, sk 2 dc; rep from * across, trc in last dc; ch 3, turn.

Row 3: Dc in each st across, ch 4, turn.

Rep Rows 2 and 3 once more. Finish off blue, join white. Continue to work in pattern by repeating Rows 2 and 3 in following color sequence:

>   * 3 rows white
>   5 rows blue

Repeat from * 6 times. At end of last row, ch 1, turn, sc in each st across. Finish off.

FRINGE

Work Single Knot Fringe (see page 16) across each short end with blue yarn. Cut 16″ strands and use 5 in each knot. Place knots every other stitch or chain across.

[CROCHETED]
Pretty Pastels
designed by Eleanor Denner

This afghan is crocheted in an unusual manner: strands of colored yarn are held together, then worked over with white yarn. The result is a lacy, textured look. It's fun and quick to do.

Size

40″ × 50″

Materials

Worsted weight yarn:
24 oz white
8 oz each of pink, yellow, blue and light green
Size Q plastic crochet hook *(or size required for gauge)*

Gauge

With 2 strands of yarn, 3 sc = 1″

Note

Throughout, work with 2 strands of white held together.

Instructions

With 2 strands of white, ch 121.

Row 1: Hold one strand each of pink, yellow, blue and green together (coming from the skeins, do not cut), and working over them, with white, sc in 2nd ch from hook and in each ch across: 120 sc; ch 1, turn.

Row 2: Continuing to work over the 4 color strands (be sure not to pull them too tightly to keep work from puckering), sc in each sc, ch 1, turn.

Rep Row 2 until afghan measures about 50″ long. Finish off, weave in all loose ends.

FRINGE

Follow Single Knot Fringe Instructions on page 16. Work Single Knot Fringe across each short end. Cut strands 18″ long, and use 5 strands (one of each color yarn) in each knot. Tie a knot in every other stitch across.

Fish Net

designed by Eleanor Denner

You may not catch a fish in this afghan, but you're sure to catch a nice catnap under its protection. Made in a pretty ombre, the big open spaces make it work up quickly.

Size

42″ × 61″

Materials

Worsted weight yarn:
 33 oz ombre
Size Q plastic crochet hook *(or size required for gauge)*

Note

Afghan is worked with 2 strands of yarn throughout.

Gauge

With 2 strands of yarn, 4 sc = 3″

Instructions

Loosely ch 55.

Row 1: Sc in 2nd ch from hook and in each ch across: 54 sc; ch 3, turn.

Row 2: Trc in next 2 sc; * ch 1, trc in next 3 sc; rep from * across, ch 3, turn.

Row 3: Trc in next 2 trc; * ch 1, trc in next 3 trc, rep from * across, ch 3, turn.

Rep Row 3 until piece measures 60″; ch 2, turn.

Last Row: Sc in each trc and in each ch-1 sp across; finish off.

FRINGE

Work Single Knot Fringe (see page 16) across each short end. Cut strands 15″ long and use 10 strands in each knot; skip one st between each knot.

Raspberry Flip

designed by Jean Leinhauser

The traditional granny square gets a new "flip" with this delightful afghan.

Size

41″ × 61″

Materials

Worsted weight yarn:
    22 oz lt pink
    12 oz dk pink
Size J aluminum crochet hook *(or size required for gauge)*
Tapestry needle

Gauge

One Square = 20″
First 2 rnds = 3½″

Instructions

SQUARE (make 6)

With dk pink, ch 5, join with a sl st to form a ring.

Rnd 1: Ch 3, 2 dc in ring; (ch 3, 3 dc in ring) 3 times; ch 3, join with a sl st to top of beg ch.

Rnd 2: Sl st across next 2 dc and into ch-3 sp; (ch 3, 2 dc, ch 3, 3 dc) all in same sp; ch 1; * in next ch-3 sp work (3 dc, ch 3, 3 dc); ch 1; rep from * twice, join with a sl st to top of beg ch 3.

Rnd 3: Sl st across next 2 dc and into ch-3 sp; ch 3, work (2 dc, ch 3, 3 dc) all in same sp; ch 1, 3 dc in next ch-1 sp for side; ch 1; * in next ch-3 sp work (3 dc, ch 3, 3 dc); ch 1; 3 dc in next ch-1 sp for side; ch 1, rep from * twice, join with a sl st to top of beg ch 3; finish off dk pink.

Rnd 4: Join lt pink in any ch-3 corner sp; ch 3; in same sp work (2 dc, ch 3, 3 dc); ch 1; * (3 dc, ch 1) in each ch-1 side sp; in next ch-3 corner sp work (3 dc, ch 3, 3 dc), ch 1; rep from * twice; (3 dc, ch 1) in each ch-1 side sp; join with a sl st to top of beg ch-3.

Rnd 5: Sl st across tops of next 2 dc and into ch-3 corner sp; ch 3; in same sp work (2 dc, ch 3, 3 dc); ch 1; * (3 dc, ch 1) in each ch-1 side sp; in next ch-3 corner sp work (3 dc, ch 3, 3 dc), ch 1; rep from * twice; (3 dc, ch 1) in each ch-1 side sp; join with a sl st to top of beg ch-3.

Rep Rnd 5 until square measures 20″. Be sure each square has the same number of rnds. Finish off, weave in ends.

EDGING

Rnd 1: With right side of square facing you, join dk pink in ch-3 sp of any outer corner; work 3 sc in sp; * sc in each st and ch-1 sp to next corner, 3 sc in corner sp; rep from * around, join with a sl st to first sc.

Rnd 2: Ch 1, sc in first sc and in next sc; 3 sc in next sc for corner; sc in each sc around, working 3 sc in center sc of each corner; join with a sl st, finish off.

JOINING

Hold two squares with right sides tog. Thread dk pink yarn into a tapestry needle. Working in outer loops only join squares along one edge, carefully matching stitches. Join a third square in same manner. Make two more strips of three squares; join all three strips.

OUTER RUFFLE

Hold afghan with right side facing you. Join dk pink with a sl st anywhere in Edging. Ch 1, sc in same sp, ch 4, sk 1 sc, * sc in next sc, ch 4, sk next sc; rep from * around, join. Finish off, weave in all ends.

Mint Frappé

designed by Jean Leinhauser

Easy to crochet, this quick afghan is cuddly and warm.

Size

41″ × 55″

Materials

Worsted weight yarn:
    25 oz mint green brushed mohair type yarn
Size N crochet hook *(or size required for gauge)*

Gauge

10 dc = 4″

Instructions

Ch 106.

Row 1: Dc in 4th ch from hook and in each ch across: 103 dc; ch 3, turn.

Row 2: Dc in each dc across; ch 3, turn.

Row 3: * (YO, insert hook into next dc and draw up a 1″ lp) 4 times (9 lps on hook), YO and draw through 8 lps, YO and draw through 2 lps: puff st made; ch 1; sk next dc; rep from * to last st (top of turning ch of last row), dc in last st. Ch 3, turn.

Row 4: * (YO, insert hook into next ch-1 sp and draw up a 1″ lp) 4 times, YO and draw through 8 lps, YO and draw through 2 lps: puff st made; ch 1; rep from * to last st, dc in last st; ch 3, turn.

Row 5: Dc in top of each puff st and in each ch-1 sp across, dc in last st; ch 3, turn.

Row 6: Dc in each dc; ch 3, turn.

Rep Rows 3 through 6 for pattern. Work in pattern until piece measures about 55″, ending by working row 6. Finish off, weave in all ends.

FRINGE

Work Single Knot Fringe (see page 16) across each short end. Cut strands 16″ long, and use 4 strands in each knot. Skip 2 sts between each knot.

[KNITTED]

Stripes on Parade

designed by Rita Weiss

What fun to knit this afghan! The stripes, made individually in long panels on size 17 needles with bulky yarn, work up very quickly.

Size

51″ × 60″ before fringing

Materials

Bulky weight yarn:
    12 ozs pink
    12 oz raspberry
    12 ozs blue
Size 17, 36″ circular knitting needle *(or size required for gauge)*
Tapestry needle

Gauge

In patt st, 2 sts = 1″

Note

Circular needle is used to accommodate large number of stitches. Do not join; work back and forth in rows.

Instructions

CENTER PANELS (make 2)

With pink, cast on 16 sts. Knit 8 rows; then work in patt as follows.

Row 1 (right side): K4; * Yo twice, K1; rep from * to last 4 sts; YO, K4: 33 sts.

Row 2: K4 * drop one YO from needle; P2; rep from * to last 5 sts; drop one YO from needle, K4: 24 sts.

Row 3: K4, K2 tog, K to last 6 sts, K2 tog, K4: 22 sts.

Row 4: K4, K2 tog, K to last 6 sts, K2 tog, K4: 20 sts.

Row 5: K4, P2 tog, P to last 6 sts, P2 tog, K4: 18 sts.

Row 6: K4, K2 tog, K to last 6 sts, K2 tog, K4: 16 sts.

Rep rows 1–6 until work measures approx 58″ from CO edge. Knit 8 rows. Bind off loosely.

MIDDLE PANELS (make 2)

With blue, work same as center panels.

END PANELS (make 2)

With raspberry, work same as center panels.

ASSEMBLING

To join, hold two center pink panels with right sides tog. Thread pink into a tapestry needle. Carefully matching sts, sew long edges tog, using overcast st. Then attach blue panels on either side in same manner. Join raspberry panels on either side of blue panels.

FRINGE

Follow Single Knot Fringe Instructions on page 16. Cut strands 16″ long and use four strands folded in half for each knot. Knot through every other stitch across short ends of afghan, matching colors of fringe to color of stripe.

Blue Leaves
designed by Rita Weiss

If leaves turned blue, they'd look like the pattern in this afghan.

Size

40″ × 60″ before fringing

Materials

Bulky weight yarn:
    24 oz blue
Size 13, 36″ circular knitting needle *(or size required for gauge)*

Gauge

In patt: 9 sts = 4″

Note

Circular needle is used to accommodate large number of stitches. Do not join; work back and forth in rows.

Instructions

Cast on 89 sts.

Row 1 (right side): K1; * YO, sl 1, K1, PSSO, K3, K2 tog, YO, K1; rep from * across.

Row 2 and all even rows: Purl.

Row 3: K2; * YO, sl 1, K1, PSSO, K1, K2 tog, YO, K3; rep from * across ending last rep with K2 instead of K3.

Row 5: P1; * K2, YO, sl 1, K2 tog, PSSO, YO, K2, P1; rep from * across.

Rows 7, 9, 11, 13 and 15: P1; * with yarn at back of work, sl 1, K1, PSSO, K1 (YO, K1) twice, K2 tog, P1; rep from * across.

Row 16: Purl.

Rep rows 1–16 until afghan measures approx 60″ ending with row 16.

Bind off loosely.

FRINGE

Follow Triple Knot Fringe Instructions on page 16. Cut strands 22″ long and use 4 strands, in each knot. Tie knot through every other cast-on or bound-off stitch across each short end of afghan.

[CROCHETED]
Anemone Floral Granny

designed by Jean Leinhauser

This pretty design is made up of four giant granny squares, crocheted with double strands of yarn on a big size Q hook. Each granny is decorated with a pretty purple flower, crocheted separately and sewn on.

Size

41″ × 44″ before fringing

Materials

Worsted weight yarn:
   6 oz Kelly Green
   12 oz White
   2 oz Purple *(for flowers)*
   8 oz Med Lavender
   ½ oz Lt Lavender *(for flowers)*

Size Q plastic crochet hook for afghan
Size J aluminum crochet hook for flowers (or sizes required for gauge)

Gauge

With Q hook and two strands of yarn,
    first two rnds of square = 6″
    completed square = 20″
With J hook and one strand of yarn,
    one completed flower = 4½″ diameter

Instructions

SQUARE (make 4)

> **Note**
> Entire square is worked with 2 strands of yarn.

With med lavender and Q hook, ch 4, join with a sl st to form a ring.

Rnd 1: Ch 3 (counts as one dc), 2 dc in ring; * ch 3 for corner, 3 dc in ring; rep from * twice more, ch 3 for corner; join with a sl st to top of beg ch-3; sl st across next 2 dc and into ch-3 sp.

Rnd 2: (Ch 3, 2 dc, ch 3 for corner, 3 dc) all in same sp; * in next corner sp work (3 dc, ch 3, 3 dc); rep from * twice more, join with a sl st to top of beg ch-3; sl st across next 2 dc and into ch-3 sp.

Rnd 3: (Ch 3, 2 dc, ch 3, 3 dc) all in same sp; * 3 dc between 3-dc groups for side; (3 dc, ch 3, 3 dc) all in next corner sp; rep from * twice, 3 dc between 3-dc groups for side, join with a sl st to top of beg ch-3; sl st across next 2 dc and into ch-3 sp.

Rnds 4 and 5: Rep Rnd 3. At end of Rnd 5, join, do not sl st. Finish off med lavender. Join green with a sl st in any corner ch-3 sp.

Rnds 6 and 7: With green, repeat Rnd 3; at end of Rnd 7, finish off green. Join white with a sl st in any corner ch-3 sp.

Rnds 8 and 9: With white, rep Rnd 3. At end of Rnd 9, finish off. Weave in all loose ends.

ASSEMBLY

Hold two squares, right sides tog, and join along one long edge, sewing with overcast st and carefully matching stitches. Join remaining two squares in same manner. Then join the two pairs of squares; the afghan is two squares wide and two squares long.

EDGING

Hold afghan with right side facing you, and join white in any outer corner sp; ch 3, dc in same sp; dc in same dc across first square, 2 dc in next corner sp; dc in seam, 2 dc in next corner sp; dc across next square to corner sp, 2 dc in corner sp; * turn work to continue along next side; now work 2 sc in side of last dc just worked; sc in each dc across first square, 2 sc in corner sp, sc in joining, 2 sc in next corner sp; sc across next square to corner, in corner work 2 sc, * ch 3, and 1 dc. Turn work to continue along next side; dc in each dc, corner sp and joining as before across 2 squares; rep from * to * once, 2 sc in side of beg ch-3, finish off; weave in all ends.

FRINGE

Work Single Knot Fringe (see page 16) across each end with the dc edging. Cut strands 16″ long and use 10 strands in each knot. Place one knot in every other dc.

FLOWERS (make 5)

> **Note**
> Flowers are worked with only one strand of yarn.

With lt lavender and J hook, ch 5, join with a sl st to form a ring.

Rnd 1: Ch 4; (dc in ring, ch 1) 10 times; join with a sl st to third ch of beg ch-4; finish off, weave in end.

Rnd 2: Join dk purple in any ch-1 sp; ch 4, 5 tr in same sp, ch 1; (in next sp work 6 tr, ch 1) 10 times; join with a sl st to top of ch-4; finish off, weave in end.

With lt lavender, sew a flower firmly in center of each square, and at center of afghan where all four squares meet.

[CROCHETED]

Lemonade

designed by Jean Leinhauser

This warm and cozy afghan would make a lovely gift.

Size

38″ × 50″

Materials

Worsted weight yarn:
    22 oz pale yellow brushed mohair type
Size K aluminum crochet hook *(or size required for gauge)*

Gauge

To check gauge, ch 24, then work first two rows of pattern; piece should measure 8″ wide.

Instructions

Ch 112.

Row 1: 3 dc in 4th ch from hook, * sk 3 chs, (sc, ch 3, 3 dc) all in next ch; rep from * across to last 4 chs, sk 3 chs, sc in last ch; ch 3, turn.

Row 2: 3 dc in base of ch, * sc under ch-3, ch 3, 3 dc under same ch-3; rep from * across, ending by working a sc in turning ch; ch 2, turn.

Rep Row 2 until piece measures 50″; finish off, weave in ends.

EDGING

Hold afghan with starting ch end at top. Join yarn with a sc in first ch-3 sp; work Row 2 across; at end, finish off. Rep at opposite end of afghan.

CHAPTER 4

HOLIDAY
Weekends

Here's a group of exciting afghans designed for the many long holiday weekends of the year. Memorial Day, Labor Day, Fourth of July, a long Christmas week—whatever the celebration, you'll find here a project that will fit your time available.

[CROCHETED]

Bright Shells

designed by Barbara Hunter

Cheerful is the word for this bright and beautiful afghan, composed of easy to make shells.

Size

39″ × 58″

Materials

Worsted weight yarn:
  8 oz white
  7 oz orange
  6 oz green
  5 oz yellow
Size J aluminum crochet hook *(or size required for gauge)*

Gauge

In pattern, 5 shells = 6″
        4 rows = 3″

Instructions

With orange, ch 109.

Row 1: Dc in 4th ch from hook and in each ch across: 107 dc (counting beg ch as a dc); ch 3, turn.

Row 2: Dc in next dc; * sk 2 dc, (shell of dc, ch 1, dc) in next dc; rep from * to last 4 sts, sk 2 dc, dc in next dc and in top of turning ch: 34 shells; ch 3, turn.

Row 3: Dc in next dc; * 4 dc in next ch-1 sp; rep from * to last 2 sts, dc in last dc, dc in turning ch sp: 34 groups of 4-dc; ch 3, turn.

Row 4: Dc in next dc, * in center of next 4-dc group (sp between first 2 dc and next 2 dc) work shell of (2 dc, ch 1, 2 dc); rep from * across, ending dc in last dc, dc in turning ch.

Row 5: Dc in next dc; * 4 dc in next ch-2 sp; rep from * to last 2 sts, dc in last dc, dc in turning ch sp: 34 groups of 4 dc; ch 3, turn.

Rows 6 through 9: Rep Rows 4 and 5. At end of Row 9, finish off orange, join white.

Rows 10 and 11: With white, rep Rows 4 and 5. At end of Row 11, finish off white, join green.

Continue to repeat Rows 4 and 5 for pattern, in following color sequence:

  2 rows green
  2 rows white
  2 rows yellow
  2 rows white
  8 rows green
  2 rows white
  2 rows yellow
  2 rows white
  2 rows orange
  2 rows white
  8 rows yellow
  2 rows white
  2 rows orange
  2 rows white
  2 rows yellow
  2 rows white
  8 rows green
  2 rows white
  2 rows yellow
  2 rows white
  2 rows green
  2 rows white
  8 rows orange

At end of last orange row, ch 3, turn.

Last Row: Dc in next 4 dc; * sk 1 dc, dc in next 3 dc; rep from * to last 3 sts, sk 1 dc, dc in last dc, dc in turning ch.

Finish off, weave in all ends.

Fourth of July Puff Stitch Afghan

designed by Rita Weiss

Make this afghan over a long July Fourth weekend. From then on, whenever you display it, there'll be no mistake as to when it was created.

Size

47″ × 60″ before fringing

Materials

Bulky weight yarn:
    18 ozs blue
    10 ozs red
    10 ozs white
Size 17, 36″ circular knitting needle *(or size required for gauge)*

Gauge

In Stock st, 2 sts = 1″

Note

Circular needle is used to accommodate large number of stitches. Do not join; work back and forth in rows.

Instructions

With blue, cast on 94 sts. Work 4 rows stock st (Knit one row; purl 1 row). Finish off blue. Join red and work in patt as follows.

Rows 1–6: Work in stock st. Finish off red. Join blue.

Row 7 (right side): K4; * slip stitch off left-hand needle and unravel this st 6 rows down to blue. Put right-hand needle through blue loop from front of work. Draw loop up and put it on left needle and knit loop off; K5; rep from * across row.

Row 8: Purl across. Finish off blue. Join white.

Rows 9–14: Work in stock st. Finish off white. Join blue.

Row 15: Repeat row 7.

Row 16: Purl across. Finish off blue; join red.

Rep rows 1–16 for pattern, 12 more times. On last rep, do not finish off blue. Work 4 rows stock st in blue.

Bind off loosely in blue. Weave in all ends.

FRINGE

Follow Single Knot Fringe Instructions on page 16. Cut strands 16″ long and use four strands in each knot. Knot through every other stitch across short ends of afghan.

[CROCHETED]

Corn on the Cob

designed by Barbara Hunter

This afghan looks as delicious as a fresh ear of corn on the cob! Alternate sections of shells and double crochet provide the texture interest.

Size

44″ × 54″ before fringing

Materials

Worsted weight yarn:
    25 oz. yellow
Size K aluminum crochet hook *(or size required for gauge)*

Gauge

8 dc = 3¼″

Instructions

Loosely ch 136.

Row 1: Sc in 2nd ch from hook and in each ch across: 135 sc; ch 3, turn (turning ch counts as first st of row throughout).

Row 2: Dc in each of next 3 sts; * sk 3 sts, shell of (4 dc, ch 1, 4 dc) all in next st; sk 3 sts, dc in next 8 sts; rep from * across to last 11 sts, sk 3 sts, shell in next st, sk 3 sts, dc in last 4 sts; ch 3, turn.

Row 3: Dc in each of next 3 dc; * ch 4, sc into ch-1 sp of shell, ch 4, dc in next 8 dc; rep from * across, ending last rep with 4 dc instead of 8; ch 3, turn.

Row 4: Dc in next 3 dc; into center sc of next group, work a shell; dc in next 8 dc; rep from * across, ending by working 4 dc instead of 8; ch 3, turn.

Rep Rows 3 and 4 for pattern. Work in pattern until piece measures 54″, ending by working Row 4; ch 1, turn.

Last Row: Sc in next 3 dc; ch 3, sc in center of group; * ch 3, sc in center of group, ch 3, sc in next 8 dc; rep from * across, ending with 4 sc. Finish off.

FRINGE

Follow Single Knot Fringe Instructions on page 16. Cut strands 16″ long and use 6 strands for each knot. Knot in center st of each shell group across each short end.

[KNITTED]

Peacock Feathers

designed by Rita Weiss

You'll be proud as a peacock when you show off this beautiful afghan. The very lacy look is created by wrapping the yarn around the needle on one row and then dropping the wraps on the next row. To keep the work neat, always gently tug on the dropped stitches in rows 3, 4, 7 and 8. Although the afghan is quick and easy to make, the adding and subtracting of wraps sometimes makes it easy to lose your place. The use of markers before each pattern repeat will eliminate this problem.

Size

40″ × 60″ before fringing

Materials

Mohair type worsted weight yarn:
    16 oz ombre
Size 13, 36″ circular needle *(or size required for gauge)*

Gauge

In patt, 10 sts = 3½″

Notes

1. Circular needle is used to accommodate large number of stitches. Do not join; work back and forth in rows.

2. Markers are merely used to indicate patt reps. Slip markers on each row.

Instructions

Cast on 108 sts. Knit 4 rows; then work in patt as follows.

Row 1: Knit.

Row 2: K4, * place marker, YO twice, K1; YO 3 times, K1; YO 4 times, K1; YO 3 times, K1; YO twice, K6; rep from * to last 4 sts, place marker, K4.

Row 3: Knit across, dropping all YO's from needle. *(Gently tug on dropped st so that it lies flat.)* Slip markers.

Row 4: Knit, slipping markers and pulling on dropped sts across row.

Row 5: Knit.

Row 6: K4, * slip marker, K6, YO twice; K1, YO 3 times; K1, YO 4 times; K1, YO 3 times; K1, YO twice; rep from * to last 4 sts, slip marker, K4.

Row 7: Rep Row 3.

Row 8: Rep Row 4.

Rep Rows 1 through 8 until afghan measures approx 60″, ending by working Row 4 or 8.

Knit 4 rows. Bind off loosely.

FRINGE

Follow Single Knot Fringe Instructions on page 16. Cut 14″ strands; use 2 strands for each knot. Tie knots evenly spaced across cast-on and bound-off ends of afghan.

[CROCHETED]
Sky Blue Pink
designed by Jean Leinhauser

A beautiful sunset spreads pink across a blue sky, and that's the feeling of complete tranquility that is expressed in this easy to make afghan.

Size

39″ × 52″

Materials

Worsted weight yarn:
    24 oz pink and blue ombre
Size J aluminum crochet hook *(or size required for gauge)*

Gauge

8 dc = 3″

Instructions

Loosely ch 106.

Row 1: Dc in 4th ch from hook; (ch 1, sk 1 ch, dc in next ch) 3 times; dc in each ch to last 7 chs, (ch 1, sk 1 ch, dc in next ch) 3 times; dc in last ch; ch 3, turn (counts as first dc of next row).

Row 2: Dc in next dc; (ch 1, sk 1 ch, dc in next dc) 3 times; dc in each dc to last 7 sts; (ch 1, sk 1 ch, dc in next dc) 3 times; dc in top of turning ch; ch 3, turn.

Rep Row 2 until piece measures 52″. Finish off. Weave in all ends.

FRINGE

Follow Single Knot Fringe Instructions on page 16. Work Single Knot Fringe across each short end. Cut strands 16″ long, and use 4 strands in each knot. Skip 2 sts between each knot.

Sky Blue Pink, p.64

Wee Bonnie Plaid, p.130

Peppermint Ripple, p.142

(L)Peppermint Stripes, p.28 / (R)Lemonade, p.54

*(L)*No Sew Granny, p.26 / *(R)*Puff Stitch Afghan, p.32

Mint Flip, p.138

*(L)*Quick Tasseled Afghan, p.88 / *(R)*Super Quick Ripple, p.34

Cuddly Kittens, p.140

Pralines 'n Cream, p.36

*(L)*Peacock Feathers, p.62 / *(R)*Angel Lace, p.22

*(L)*Fish Net, p.42 / *(R)*Café au Lait, p.24

Northern Lights, p.106

Roman Stripes, p.108

Fisherman Ripple, p.124

*(L)*Raspberry Flip, p.44 / *(R)*Mint Frappé, p.46

Anemone Floral Granny, p.52

Fire and Flames, p.122

San Diego Sunset, p.116

Freedom Ripple, p.98

(L)Midshipman, p.38
(R)Fourth of July Puff Stitch Afghan, p.58

Ocean Waves, p.86

Square at a Time, p.112

Scarlet Ribbons, p.134

*(L)*Desert Stripes, p.120 / *(R)*Golden Sunshine, p.118

Waves of Autumn, p.100

Yesterday's Granny, p.110

Flame Ripple, p.96

*(L)*Corn on the Cob, p.60 / *(C)*Pumpkin Shell, p.20 / *(R)*Pastel Rainbow, p.104

Roses in the Snow, p.92

Sweet Sherbet, p.128

Baby Cables, p.132

Buttercup, p.129

Surf's Up Granny, p.90

*(L)*Bright Shells, p.56 / *(R)*Autumn Leaves, p.102

*(L)*Self-Fringing Afghan, p.30
*(R)*Front Post, Back Post, p.94

Tomorrow's Heirloom, p.84

Shell Stitch, p.136

Surf's Up Granny, p.90

*(L)*Bright Shells, p.56 / *(R)*Autumn Leaves, p.102

*(L)*Self-Fringing Afghan, p.30
*(R)*Front Post, Back Post, p.94

Tomorrow's Heirloom, p.84

Shell Stitch, p.136

*(L)*Pretty Pastels, p.40 / *(R)*Blue Sky, p.82

*(L)*Stripes on Parade, p.48 / *(R)*Blue Leaves, p.50

*(L)*Toasty Warm, p.81 / *(R)*Dusty Rose Shells, p.126

Carriage Trade, p.103

Pretty Patchwork, p. 114

80

[KNITTED]

Toasty Warm

designed by Rita Weiss

Because it's made with bulky yarn, this afghan will be warm as toast. Start it as soon as the weatherman begins to predict a cold spell coming, and because it is worked on large needles, you'll have it finished just in time.

Size

37″ × 60″ before fringing

Materials

Brushed bulky weight yarn:
    22 ozs ombre
Size 13, 36″ circular knitting needle *(or size required for gauge)*

Note

Circular needle is used to accommodate large number of stitches. Do not join; work back and forth in rows.

Gauge

In garter st, 5 sts = 2″

Instructions

Loosely cast on 93 sts.

Rows 1−4: Knit

Rows 5, 7, 9 and 11 (right side): K5 * (K2 tog) twice; (YO, K1) 3 times; YO (sl 1, K1, PSSO) twice, K1 *; rep from * to * 6 times, K4.

Rows 6, 8, 10 and 12: K4, purl to last 4 sts, K4.

Rep rows 1−12 until afghan measures approx 58″, ending by working row 12.

Work 6 rows of garter st (knit each row). Bind off loosely.

FRINGE

Follow Basic Fringe Instructions on page 16 and make Spaghetti Fringe. Cut 14″ strands. Knot one strand in each st across both short ends of afghan.

Blue Sky

designed by Jean Leinhauser

Granny squares work up very quickly to create a beautiful afghan that is sure to become a family heirloom.

Size

42″ × 56″

Materials

Worsted weight yarn:
    30 oz light blue
Size J aluminum crochet hook *(or size required for gauge)*

Gauge

One 5-rnd square = 7″

Instructions

SQUARE (make 48)

Ch 6, join with a sl st to form a ring.

Rnd 1: Ch 3; (YO, insert hook in ring and draw up a ½″ lp, YO and draw through 2 lps on hook) twice; YO and draw through all 3 lps on hook: first petal made; * ch 5, (YO, insert hook in ring and draw up a ½″ lp, YO and draw through 2 lps on hook) 3 times; YO and draw through all 4 lps on hook: another petal made; ch 1, work a petal; rep from * twice, ch 5, petal; ch 1, join with a sl st to top of first petal.

Rnd 2: Sl st into next ch-5 sp, work first petal as before in same sp; ch 3, work another petal in same sp (first corner made); * ch 1, 3 dc in next ch-1 sp, ch 1; in next ch-5 sp work (petal, ch 3, petal) (second corner made); rep from * twice, ch 1, 3 dc in next sp, ch 1, join to top of first petal.

Rnd 3: Sl st in next ch-3 sp, work first corner as before in same sp; * ch 2, dc in next ch-1 sp, dc in next 3 dc, dc in next sp, ch 2; work corner sp as before in next sp; rep from * twice, ch 2, dc in next sp, dc in next 3 dc, dc in next sp, ch 2, join.

Rnd 4: Sl st into next ch-3 sp, work first corner in same sp; * ch 2, dc in next sp and in each dc to next sp, dc in sp, ch 2; work corner in next sp; rep from * twice, ch 2, dc in next sp, dc in each dc to next sp, dc in sp, ch 2, join.

Rnd 5: Rep Rnd 4. Finish off, weave in ends.

JOINING

To join, hold two squares with right sides facing. Sew together with overcast st, working in outer lps only, taking care to match stitches. Make 8 strips of 6 squares each; then join strips in same manner. With right side of afghan facing, join yarn in any outer corner sp, and work one row sc around, working 3 sc in every outer corner sp.

FRINGE

Follow Single Knot Fringe Instructions on page 16. Work Single Knot fringe across both short ends. Cut strands 15″ long, and use 6 strands in each knot. Skip 2 sts between each knot.

[KNITTED]
Tomorrow's Heirloom
designed by Barbara Hunter

Whip up this quick afghan today. It's sure to be a family favorite forever.

Size

44″ × 60″ before fringing

Materials

Worsted weight yarn:
    20 ozs ombre
Size 15, 36″ circular knitting needle *(or size required for gauge)*

Gauge

In stock st, 5 sts = 2″

Instructions

Cast on 113 sts.

Row 1: K5, * sl 1, K5. Rep from * across row.

Row 2: P5, * sl 1, P5. Rep from * across row.

Row 3: Rep Row 1.

Row 4: Purl.

Rep Rows 1–4 for pattern until afghan measures approx 60″, ending by working Row 4. Bind off loosely. Steam ends lightly.

FRINGE

Follow Triple Knot Fringe Instructions on page 16. Cut strands 25″ long and use 8 strands for each knot. Tie knot in every fourth cast-on or bound-off stitch across both short ends of afghan.

[CROCHETED]

Ocean Waves

designed by Eleanor Denner

This extra easy pattern is also extra quick. It's worked on a big size Q plastic hook for when time is short. The afghan would also be pretty worked in a solid color.

Size

45″ × 60″

Materials

Worsted weight yarn:
    30 oz. ombre
Size Q plastic crochet hook *(or size required for gauge)*

Gauge

With two strands of yarn, in pattern 6 sts = 4″

Instructions

Ch 55.

Row 1: Sc in 2nd ch from hook, hdc in next ch, dc in next ch; * sc in next ch, hdc in next ch, dc in next ch; rep from * across; ch 1, turn.

Row 2: * Sc in dc, hdc in hdc, dc in sc; rep from * across, ch 1, turn.

Rep Row 2 until work measures about 60″. Finish off, weave in all ends.

FRINGE

Follow Single Knot Fringe Instructions on page 16. Work Single Knot Fringe across each short end. Cut strands 18″ long and use 5 strands in each knot. Tie a knot in every other st.

[KNITTED]
Quick Tasseled Afghan

This beautiful afghan is made on circular needles to accommodate the large number of stitches. You'll use two sizes (7 and 17) to create the pretty "puffed" effect. The yarn is beautiful, soft Paton's Diana, which has a lovely brushed finish.

Size

45" × 54"

Materials

Paton's Diana yarn (50 gr. balls)
    6 white (Main color—abbrev MC)
    6 medium pink (Contrast Color A)
    5 dark pink (Contrast Color B)
Susan Bates® 29" long circular knitting needles, sizes 7 and 17 (or sizes required for gauge)
Susan Bates® Adjustable "Trim Tool"™

Gauge

On larger needle in stock st,
    10 sts = 4"
    10 rows = 4"
On smaller needle in pattern,
    12¾ sts = 4"
    4 rows = ¾"

Notes

1. The abbreviation "M1" means to make one st by picking up the horizontal strand lying before next st, then working into back of it.

2. The afghan is worked from side to side.

Instructions

With smaller needle and MC, loosely cast on 216 sts; do not join, work back and forth in rows.

BORDER

Rows 1 through 5: Knit.

Row 6: * K3, K2 tog; rep from * to last st, K1: 173 sts. Cut MC.

Now work in stripe pattern as follows:

Rows 1–8: With larger needle and Color A, work in St st (K1 row, P 1 row), beg with a K row. Cut A.

Rows 9–12: With smaller needle and MC, work in St st, beg with a K row. Cut MC.

Rows 13–20: With larger needle and B, work in St st, beg with a K row. Cut B.

Rows 21–24: With smaller needle and MC, work in St st, beg with a K row. Cut MC.

Rep Rows 1–24 four more times, then rep Rows 1–8 once more.

Next Row: With smaller needle and MC, * K4, M1; rep from * to last st, K1: 216 sts. K5 rows for border. Bind off loosely.

FINISHING

With "Trim Tool" and MC, make 24, 4" tassels wrapping yarn 30 times. Attach to each end of each MC stripe, allowing ends of afghan to turn under.

[CROCHETED]

Surf's Up Granny

designed by Eleanor Denner

This unusual granny combines two solid colors with an unusual ombre that looks like the white, aquamarine and blue of ocean surf. Change the colors as you wish to match any pretty ombre you find.

Size

40″ × 60″ before fringing

Materials

Worsted weight yarn:
 8 oz bright blue
 8 oz white
 28 oz ombre
Size K aluminum crochet hook *(or size required for gauge)*

Gauge

With two strands of yarn,
 5 dc = 2″
 first 5 rnds = 8½″
 square = 20″

Note
Work with two strands of yarn throughout.

Instructions

SQUARE (make 6)

With blue, ch 5, join with a sl st to form a ring.

Rnd 1: Ch 3, 2 dc in ring; (ch 5, 3 dc in ring) 3 times; ch 5, join to top of beg ch-3 with a sl st.

Rnd 2: Ch 3, dc in next 2 dc; * (2 dc, ch 5, 2 dc) in next ch-5 sp; dc in next 3 dc; rep from * twice; (2 dc, ch 5, 2 dc) in last ch-5 sp; join with a sl st to top of beg ch-3; finish off blue.

Rnd 3: Join white in any ch-5 corner sp; (ch 3, dc, ch 5, 2 dc) all in same sp; * dc in each dc to corner, in corner ch-5 sp work (2 dc, ch 5, 2 dc); rep from * twice, dc in each dc; join with a sl st to top of beg ch-3.

Rnds 4 and 5: Continuing with white, work in pattern around. At end of Rnd 5, finish off white.

Rnd 6: With ombre, rep Rnd 3.

Rnd 7 through 12: Continuing with ombre, work in pattern around. At end of Rnd 12, finish off ombre.

ASSEMBLY

Join squares in 2 rows of 3 squares each. To join, hold squares with right sides together. Working with one strand of ombre yarn, join with sc working in outer lps only. Carefully match stitches, and don't work too tightly. With ombre, work one rnd sc all around afghan.

FRINGE

Fringe each short end with Single Knot Fringe (see page 16). Cut strands of white 18″ long, and use 6 strands in each knot. Tie knots in sc sts, skipping 1 sc between each knot.

Roses in the Snow
designed by Eleanor Denner

Choose your favorite color to center the striking white motifs that make up this lovely afghan.

Size

50″ × 67″

Materials

Worsted weight yarn:
- 4 oz Rose
- 24 oz White

Size K aluminum crochet hook *(or size required for gauge)*

Gauge

One Full Motif = 9″ (measured side to side)

Instructions

FULL MOTIF (make 32)

With rose, ch 6, join with a sl st to form a ring.

Rnd 1: Ch 4, 2 trc in ring; * ch 3, 3 trc in ring; rep from * 5 times, join with a sl st to top of beg ch-4, finish off rose.

Rnd 2: Join white with a sl st in any ch-3 sp; (ch 4, 2 trc, ch 3, 3 trc) all in same sp; * (3 trc, ch 3, 3 trc) all in next ch-3 sp; rep from * 5 times, join with a sl st in top of beg ch-4.

Rnd 3: Sl st across next 2 trc and into ch-3 sp; ch 4, (2 trc, ch 3, 3 trc) all in same sp for corner; between next two 3 trc groups, work 3 trc for side; * in next ch-3 sp, work (3 trc, ch 3, 3 trc) for corner; between next two 3 trc groups, work 3 trc for side; rep from * 5 times, join with a sl st to top of beg ch-4.

Rnds 4 and 5: Rep Rnd 3, adding one side group on each rnd. At end of Rnd 5, finish off.

SIDE MOTIFS (make 6)

With white, ch 18.

Row 1: 2 trc in 4th ch from hook, trc in each ch to last ch, 3 trc in last ch; ch 4, turn.

Rows 2 through 5: Trc in first st, trc in each st to last st, 2 trc in top of turning ch. At end of Row 5, finish off.

FINISHING

Weave in all loose ends.

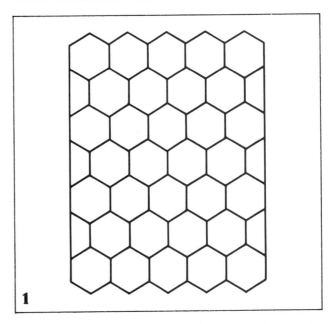

Sew squares and side motifs together, as shown in **Fig. 1.** To sew, hold with right sides tog, and work in overcast st in back lps only, carefully matching stitches.

EDGING

Row 1: With right side of afghan facing, join white with a sl st in any outer corner ch-3 sp; sc in each st around, working 3 sc in every outer corner sp; join with a sl st.

Row 2: * Sc in next sc, ch 3; rep from * around, join, finish off.

Front Post, Back Post
designed by Eleanor Denner

This light weight afghan gets the interesting texture of its design by stitches worked around the post of the stitch below. It's fun to make in three colors with a big K hook.

Size

48″ × 60″

Materials

Worsted weight yarn:
    8 oz rust
    8 oz slate blue
    4 oz white
Size K aluminum crochet hook *(or size required for gauge)*

Special Techniques

This pattern uses two stitches that may be unfamiliar to you: both are worked around the post of a trc, one from the back and one from the front. To work a Back Post trc (abbreviated BPtrc) refer to **Fig 1** for diagram and instructions; to work a Front Post trc (abbreviated FPtrc), refer to **Fig 2**.

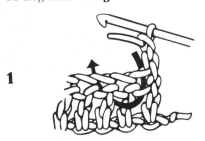

1

BACK POST TRC (abbreviated BPtrc). YO hook twice, insert hook from back to front around post of trc in row below; YO, draw yarn through; complete as for a regular trc.

2

FRONT POST TRC (abbreviated FPtrc). YO hook twice, insert hook from front to back around post of trc in row below; YO, draw yarn through; complete as for a regular trc.

Gauge

7 dc = 2″

Instructions

With blue, loosely ch 152.

Row 1: Trc in 6th ch from hook; * ch 1, sk 1 ch, trc in next ch; rep from * across, ch 4, turn.

Row 2: FPtrc in next trc, ch 1, FPtrc in next 3 trc; * (ch 1, trc in next trc) 5 times; (FPtrc, ch 1) in next 5 trc; rep from * across, ending with 5 FPtrc; ch 4, turn.

Row 3: Work same as Row 2, but work BPtrc in place of each FPtrc.

Row 4: Rep Row 2.

Row 5: Rep Row 3.

These 5 rows complete one pattern. You now will reverse the pattern by working trc sts where post sts were worked before, and post sts in the trc sections.

Work two more patterns with blue, reversing as above each time the pattern changes. This completes 15 rows of blue.

Change to white and work one pattern (5 rows).

Change to rust and work 5 patterns (25 rows).

Change to white and work 1 pattern (5 rows).

Change to blue and work 3 patterns (15 rows).

Finish off, weave in all ends.

EDGING

Rnd 1: Hold afghan with last row worked at top. Join rust with a sl st in upper right-hand corner; ch 3, 4 dc in same sp; dc in each st and in each ch-1 sp across top, work 5 dc in next corner; 2 dc in each row and 1 dc in each st along side, 5 dc in next corner; work across bottom as for top, 5 dc in corner, work second side same as first; join with a sl st to top of beg ch. Finish off rust.

Rnd 2: Join white in center st of any outer corner sp; (ch 6, dc, ch 3, dc) all in same st; ch 3; sk 1 dc; * dc in next dc, ch 1, sk next dc; rep from * around, working (dc, ch 3) 3 times in each corner center st. Join, finish off white.

Rnd 3: Join blue in any outer corner center st; ch 3, 2 dc in same st; dc in each dc and ch-1 sp around, working 3 dc in each outer corner st. Finish off, weave in all ends.

[KNITTED]
Flame Ripple

Curl up by the fire under this cozy afghan, worked with a dropped wrap stitch that works up in a jiffy.

Size

42″ × 56″ before fringing

Materials

Dawn Sayelle knitting worsted weight yarn:
    8 oz Amber
    12 oz Orange
    12 oz Burnt Orange
Size 11, 29″ circular knitting needle (*or size required for gauge*)

Gauge

In stock st, 7 sts = 2″

Instructions

With Orange, cast on 172 sts loosely. Do not join; work back and forth in rows.

Row 1 (right side): Purl.

Row 2: Knit.

Row 3: Purl. Finish off Orange; Join Burnt Orange.

Row 4: With Burnt Orange, P2, * P2 tog; P17, P2 tog through back lps; rep from * to last 2 sts, P2 = 156 sts.

Row 5: Purl.

Row 6: P2; * P2 tog, P15, P2 tog through back lps; rep from * to last 2 sts, P2 = 140 sts. Finish off Burnt Orange; join Amber.

Row 7: With Amber, K2; * sl 1 as to knit, K1, PSSO; K13, K2 tog; rep from * to last 2 sts, K2 = 124 sts.

Row 8: Knit.

Row 9: * K5, work (YO twice, K1) 10 times; rep from * to last 4 sts, K4.

Row 10: * K5, (knit first YO, drop next YO, K1) 10 times; rep from * to last 4 sts, K4 = 204 sts. Finish off Amber; join Burnt Orange.

Row 11: With Burnt Orange, K2; * sl 1 as to knit, K1, PSSO; K21, K2 tog; rep from * to last 2 sts, K2 = 188 sts.

Row 12: Purl.

Row 13: Purl. Finish off Burnt Orange; join Orange.

Row 14: With Orange, P2; * P2 tog, P19, P2 tog through back lps; rep from * to last 2 sts, P2 = 172 sts.

Rep Rows 1 through 14 until afghan measures approx 56″ long, ending by working Row 2. Bind off all sts loosely in purl. Weave in all ends.

FRINGE

Following Spaghetti Fringe instructions on page 16, fringe each short end of afghan. Cut 10″ strands of Orange. Using one strand for each knot of fringe, tie one knot in each st. across.

[CROCHETED]
Freedom Ripple

It may be hot over the Fourth of July Weekend, but if you get started then on this patriotic afghan, you'll be grateful when winter's cool winds start to blow!

Size

44″ × 54″

Materials

Dawn Sayelle knitting worsted weight yarn:
- 20 oz Baby Blue
- 12 oz True Blue
- 8 oz Flame
- 8 oz White

Size K aluminum crochet hook (or size required for gauge)

Gauge

In sc, 3 sts = 1″

Instructions

With True Blue, ch 176 loosely.

Row 1 (foundation row—right side): Sc in 2nd ch from hook, sk one ch, sc in each of next 4 chs. * Work 3 sc in next ch (for point), sc in each of next 3 chs; sk 2 chs, sc in each of next 3 chs; rep from * to last 7 chs. Work 3 sc in next ch (for last point), sc in each of next 4 chs; sk one ch, sc in last ch.

Row 2 (patt row): Ch 1, turn; sc in first sc, sk one sc, sc in each of next 4 sc. * Work 3 sc in next sc (center sc of 3-sc group at point), sc in each of next 3 sc; sk 2 sc, sc in each of next 3 sc; rep from * to last 7 sc. Work 3 sc in next sc (center sc of 3-sc group at last point), sc in each of next 4 sc; sk one sc, sc in last sc.

Row 3: Rep Row 2, changing to White in last sc. [To Change Colors: Work last st until 2 lps rem on hook; finish off, leaving approx 4″ end. With new color (leave 4″ end), complete st (YO and draw through both lps on hook) = color changed.] (At beg of next row, work over yarn ends for several sts.)

Row 4: With White, rep Row 2, changing to Flame in last sc.

Row 5: With Flame (remember to work over yarn ends), rep Row 2, changing to Baby Blue in last sc.

Row 6: With Baby Blue, rep Row 2.

Row 7 (PC row): Continuing with Baby Blue, ch 2, turn; sk first sc, dc in each of next 3 sc, work PC (popcorn) in next sc [To Make PC: Work 4 dc in st; remove hook from lp and insert in first dc of 4-dc group just made; hook dropped lp and pull through lp on hook, ch 1 tightly = PC made], dc in next sc. * Work 3 dc in next sc (center sc of 3 sc-group at point), dc in next sc; PC in next sc, work CL (cluster) over next 4 sc [To Make CL: Work (YO, insert hook in next sc and draw up a lp, YO and draw through 2 lps on hook) 4 times (5 lps now on hook); YO and draw through all 5 lps on hook = CL made]; PC in next sc, dc in next sc; rep from * to last 7 sc. Work 3 dc in next sc (center sc of 3-sc group at last point), dc in next sc; PC in next sc, dc in each of next 2 sc; work dc dec (decrease) over last 2 sc as follows: Work (YO, insert hook in next sc and draw up a lp, YO and draw through 2 lps on hook) twice (3 lps now on hook); YO and draw through all 3 lps on hook = dc dec made.

Row 8: Continuing with Baby Blue, ch 1, turn; sc in first st (dc dec), sk next dc, sc in next dc; sc in PC (work in dc where dropped lp was pulled through), sc in each of next 2 dc. * Work 3 sc in next dc (center dc of 3-dc group at point), sc in each of next 2 dc; sc in PC, sk cluster, sc in next PC; sc in each of next 2 dc; rep from * to last point. Work 3 sc in next dc (center dc of 3-dc group at last point), sc in each of next 2 dc; sc in next PC, sc in next dc, sk next dc; sc in last dc, changing to Flame. (Ch-2 at end of row is left unworked.)

Row 9: With Flame, rep Row 2, changing to White in last sc.

Row 10: With White, rep Row 2, changing to True Blue in last sc.

Rep Rows 1 through 10, 10 times more; then rep Rows 1 through 3 once more. At end of last row, do not change to White. Finish off; weave in ends. Lightly steam press edges on wrong side to prevent curling.

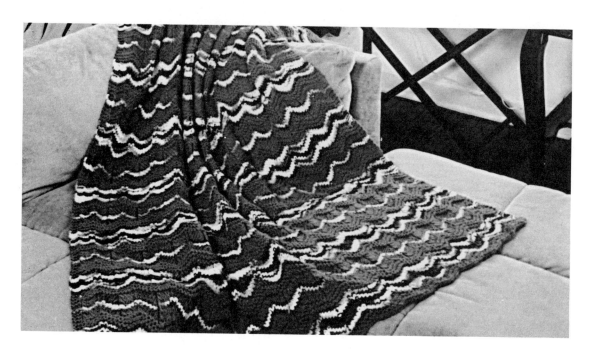

Waves of Autumn

Remember the smell of leaves burning, the days of Indian Summer? This afghan brings all those wonderful autumn days to mind.

Size

44″ × 54″

Materials

Dawn Sayelle knitting worsted weight yarn:
  18 oz Country Red
  10 oz Tiger Lily Ombre
  4 oz Rust
Size 11, 36″ circular knitting needle *(or size required for gauge)*

Gauge

In garter st (knit each row), 7 sts = 2″

Instructions

With Country Red, cast on 182 sts loosely. Do not join; work back and forth in rows.

Rows 1 through 5: With Country Red, knit 5 rows. At end of Row 5, finish off Country Red; join Tiger Lily.

Row 6 (right side): With Tiger Lily, K3; * K2 tog, K2; knit in front and back in each of next 2 sts (2 sts increased), K3; sl 1, K1, PSSO; rep from * to last 3 sts, K3.

Row 7: K3, purl to last 3 sts, K3.

Rows 8 and 9: Rep Rows 6 and 7. At end of Row 9, drop Tiger Lily (do not cut); join Rust.

Rows 10 and 11: With Rust, rep Rows 6 and 7. At end of Row 11, finish off Rust; continue with Tiger Lily (bring color up side of work).

Rows 12 through 15: With Tiger Lily, rep Rows 6 and 7, twice (4 rows total). At end of Row 15, finish off Tiger Lily; join Country Red.

Row 16: With Country Red, rep Row 6.

Rows 17 through 21: Knit 5 rows.

Rows 22 through 25: Continuing with Country Red, rep Rows 6 and 7, twice (4 rows total). At end of Row 25, drop Country Red (do not cut); join Tiger Lily.

Rows 26 and 27: With Tiger Lily, rep Rows 6 and 7. At end of Row 27, finish off Tiger Lily; continue with Country Red (bring color up side of work).

Rows 28 through 32: With Country Red, rep Rows 6 and 7, twice; then rep Row 6 once more (5 rows total).

Rep Rows 1 through 32, six times more; then rep Rows 1 through 16 once. Continuing with Country Red, knit 4 more rows. Bind off all sts loosely in knit. Finish off; weave in all ends. Lightly steam press on wrong side.

CHAPTER 5

LOST
Weekends

Lost in a knitting or crochet project, that is. These are for the weekends that sort of slip on into next week. You're so lost in the new project that you forget Monday's here . . . or Tuesday . . . or . . . Well, turn off the phone, pull down the shades, tell everyone you're out of town.

This group does take more time, but the results will be worth it.

[CROCHETED]

Autumn Leaves

designed by Eleanor Denner

The lovely rust shade of autumn leaves is used in this afghan; try a spring green yarn for a fresh spring look; or a bright red to herald the Christmas holiday season.

Size

41″ × 55″ before fringing

Materials

Worsted weight yarn:
    28 oz rust
Size K aluminum crochet hook *(or size required for gauge)*

Gauge

3 shells = 4″

Instructions

Ch 146 loosely.

Row 1: Trc in 4th ch from hook and in next 2 chs; sk 2 chs, sl st in next ch; * ch 3, trc in next 2 chs, sk 2 chs, sl st in next ch; rep from * across to last 2 chs, sk 1 ch, trc in last ch; turn.

Row 2: Sl st across tops of next 2 trc and into ch-3 sp; * ch 3, 2 trc in same sp; sl st into next ch-3 sp; rep from * to last ch-3 sp, ch 3, 2 trc in same sp; turn.

Rep Row 3 until work measures 55″. Finish off.

Hold afghan with starting chain at top. Join yarn and rep Row 1 across chain. Finish off.

FRINGE

Make Single Knot Fringe (see page 16) across each short end. Cut strands 16″ long and use 8 strands in each knot. Place one knot in each ch-3 sp.

[KNITTED]

Carriage Trade

Size

48″ × 57″

Materials

Coats & Clark Red Heart 4 ply handknitting yarn:

- 14 ozs Off White (#3)
- 7 ozs Paddy Green (#686)
- 7 ozs Amethyst (#588)
- 7 ozs Burnt Orange (#255)
- 7 ozs Dk Turquoise (#515)

Size 10, 36″ circular knitting needle (*or size required for gauge*)

Gauge

1 scallop (18 sts) = 4″
4 stripes (20 rows) = 3½″

Note

A circular needle is recommended to accommodate the large number of sts. Do not join. Work in rows.

Instructions

Starting at narrow edge, with Orange cast on 216 sts. K3 rows. Now work as follows.

Row 1 (right side): (K1, YO) 3 times; * (K2 tog) 6 times; (K1, YO) 6 times. Rep from * to last 15 sts, (K2 tog) 6 times; (YO, K1) 3 times.

Row 2: Counting each YO as a st and knitting in back of every YO, K across: 216 sts. Break off Orange, attach White.

Rows 3–6: With White work in stockinette st (K1 row, P1 row). Break off White, attach Amethyst.

Rows 7–8: Rep Rows 1 and 2.

Rows 9–10: K across.

Rows 11–12: Rep Rows 1 and 2. At end of last row break off Amethyst, attach White.

Repeating Rows 3–12 for stitch pattern throughout, work

- 4 rows White
- 6 rows Turquoise
- 4 rows White
- 6 rows Green
- 4 rows White

—8 color stripes completed. Starting with Orange, rep last 8 stripes 7 times more; then work 4 rows Orange.

Next Row: K across. Bind off.

[CROCHETED]
Pastel Rainbow
designed by Barbara Hunter

Six beautiful colors are combined with white to make the soft pastel look of this rainbow afghan. The pretty Puff Stitch pattern makes it light and fluffy.

Size

42″ × 54″ before fringing

Materials

Mohair type worsted weight yarn:
- 12 oz White *(Color A)*
- 3 oz Crystal Lilac *(Color B)*
- 3 oz Frosty Mint *(Color C)*
- 3 oz Orange Ice *(Color D)*
- 3 oz Pale Yellow *(Color E)*
- 3 oz Pink *(Color F)*
- 3 oz Sky Blue *(Color G)*

Size K aluminum crochet hook *(or size required for gauge)*

Gauge

3 puff sts and 2 sc = 2″ (measured across center)

Note

To change color at end of a dc row:

Work across, draw up a loop in last st (3 loops on hook); YO, draw through 2 loops, change to new color, YO, draw through rem 2 loops; ch 2, turn.

Puff Stitch Pattern (PS)

(YO hook, insert hook in stitch, draw up a long loop) 3 times, YO and through all 7 loops on hook.

Instructions

With Color A, ch 104 loosely.

Foundation Row: Sc in 2nd ch from hook and in each ch across: 103 sc; ch 2, turn.

Row 1: Skip first sc, dc in next sc; * ch 1, sk 1 sc, PS in next sc; rep from * across, ending dc in last sc, dc in top of ch-2, ch 2, turn.

Row 2: Skip first st, dc in next dc; * PS in ch-1 sp, ch 1; rep from * across ending PS in 3rd st from end, dc in last dc, dc in top of ch-2; ch 2, turn.

Row 3: Rep Row 2.

Rows 2 and 3 comprise 1 Pattern Row. Work 7 pattern rows following color sequence below.

7 pattern rows EACH of A, B, A, C, A, D, A, E, A, F, A, G, A.

Fasten off, weave in all loose ends.

FRINGE

Follow Single Knot Fringe Instructions on page 16. Cut strands of each color, 16″ long. Use 4 strands of one color in each knot, and tie knot through the space between each Puff Stitch across each short end of afghan.

Northern Lights

designed by Barbara Hunter

Like the blaze of a northern night, this beautiful afghan takes more time to make, but the result is well worth the effort.

Size

40″ × 54″ before fringing

Materials

Worsted weight yarn:
    6 oz White *(Color A)*
    4 oz Gray *(Color B)*
    4 oz Black *(Color C)*
    4 oz Scarlet *(Color D)*
Size K aluminum crochet hook *(or size required for gauge)*

Gauge

5 sc = 2″
4 rows = 1″

Special Notes

1. Long sc: This special stitch is used to create the bargello effect. To work it, single crochet at base of next sc 2, 3 or 4 rows below; keep the long stitches loose so afghan won't draw up.

2. To change color at end of a sc row, draw up a loop in last st (2 loops on hook), change to new color, YO, draw through both loops; ch 1, turn.

Instructions

With Color A, ch 103 sts loosely.

Row 1: Sc in 2nd ch from hook and in each ch across; ch 1, turn.

Rows 2 through 4: Sc in each sc across; ch 1, turn. At end of Row 4, attach Color B at last sc. Finish off Color A, leaving a 4″ tail for weaving later; ch 1, turn.

Row 5: With Color B, sc in first sc; * 1 long sc in next st 2 rows below (in Row 3), 1 long sc in next st 3 rows below (in Row 2); 1 long sc in next st 4 rows below (in Row 1); 1 long sc in next st 3 rows below, 1 long sc in next st 2 rows below, sc in next sc; rep from * across; ch 1, turn.

Rows 6 through 8: Sc in each sc across; ch 1, turn. At end of Row 8, attach Color C at last sc. Finish off Color B, leaving a 4″ tail for weaving later; ch 1, turn.

Rows 9 through 12: With Color C, rep Rows 5 through 8. At end of Row 8, attach Color D at last sc. Finish off Color C, leaving a 4″ tail for weaving later; ch 1, turn.

Rows 13 through 16: With color D, rep Rows 5 through 8.

Alternating 4 rows each of A, B, C, D, rep Rows 5 through 8 in pattern until piece measures 54″, ending with 4 rows of Color A. Weave in all loose ends.

FRINGE

Follow Single Knot Fringe Instructions on page 16. Cut strands of each color, 16″ long. Using 2 strands for each knot, knot in every 4th stitch across each short end of afghan. Knot in this color sequence: * White, Gray, Black, Red; rep from * across.

[CROCHETED]

Roman Stripes

designed by Barbara Hunter

Bright stripes of fresh colors make this an exciting afghan. Fringe is worked as you go, by leaving a long yarn end at beginning and end of each row. These ends are then braided into clever little pigtails for fringe.

Size

40″ × 56″

Materials

Worsted weight yarn:
    4 oz each of:
        Kelly Green *(Color A)*
        Bright Yellow Green *(Color B)*
        Lavender *(Color C)*
        Purple *(Color D)*
        Lt Turquoise *(Color E)*
        Dk Turquoise *(Color F)*
        Bright Med Turquoise *(Color G)*
        Dark Blue *(Color H)*
        White *(Color J)*
Size K aluminum crochet hook *(or size required for gauge)*

Gauge

In sc, 3 sts = 1″
    5 rows = 2½″

Notes

1. Each row is worked separately; do not turn work. Finish off after every row.

2. To begin each row: Leave a yarn tail of 9″. Make a slip knot on hook; remove hook, insert hook into first stitch of previous row and pull slip knot through; ch 1. Then continue in sc across row.

3. To end each row: at end of last st, cut yarn 8″ from hook, pull tail through loop on hook.

4. Work in back loop only (loop away from you) throughout.

Instructions

With Color A, loosely ch 169 (remember to leave 9″ yarn end at beg of ch, and 8″ yarn end at end of row).

Row 1: Continuing with Color A and following notes above, join yarn at beg of row, sc in each ch across, finish off.

Row 2: With B, join yarn at beg of row, sc in each sc across, finish off.

Rep Row 2, in following color sequence:

    1 row Color B
    *1 row Color J
    2 rows Color C
    2 rows Color D
    1 row Color J
    2 rows Color E
    2 rows Color F
    1 row Color J
    2 rows Color G
    2 rows Color H
    1 row Color J *
    2 rows Color A
    2 rows Color B

Rep from * to * one more time.

Now work:

    2 rows Color A
    2 rows Color B
    1 row Color J
    2 rows Color C
    2 rows Color D
    1 row Color J
    1 row Color E
    1 row Color F
    1 row Color G
    1 row Color H
    1 row Color J

You have now completed one half of the afghan. Continue in same manner, working in exact reverse color sequence (1 row Color J, H, G, F, E, and J, 2 rows Color D, etc.).

End with 2 rows of Color A.

FINISHING

Starting at one end of afghan, pick up all strands of Colors A, B and J and braid loosely so afghan does not pucker. Braid to about 2″ from end, use one strand from braid to tie twice around braid and knot. This will secure end. Continue across, using in each braid two colors and white. Continue to center section where there are single rows of colors. Braid the three turquoise sections; a blue, white and blue section; then three turquoise again; then continue as before across.

Repeat at other end of afghan.

[CROCHETED]
Yesterday's Granny

Size

53″ × 72″

Materials

Coats & Clark Red Heart 4 ply handknitting yarn:
  25 oz Black
  25 oz Burnt Orange
  11 oz Orange
  11 oz Yellow
Size I Aluminum Crochet Hook (or size required for gauge)
Scraps of blue and green yarn to use for markers.

Gauge

Motif is 8½″ square without stripes. Each panel measures 8½″ × 71″.

Instructions

PANEL (make 6)

Motif A with Stripe Section: Starting at center, with Burnt Orange ch 6. Join with sl st to form ring.

Rnd 1: Ch 3, 15 dc in ring. Join to top of ch-3. With blue mark this rnd.

Rnd 2: Ch 3, 2 dc in joining, (ch 1, sk 1 dc; in next

dc make 3 dc, ch 3 and 3 dc—corner group made; ch 1, sk 1 dc, 3 dc in next dc) 3 times; ch 1, sk 1 dc; corner group in next dc; ch 1. Join to top of ch-3. Fasten off.

Rnd 3: Attach Yellow to any ch-3 corner sp; ch 3, in same sp make 2 dc, ch 3 and 3 dc—starting corner group made; * ch 1, (2 dc in next ch-1 sp, ch 1) twice; corner group in ch-3 corner sp. Rep from * 2 more times; ch 1, (2 dc in next ch-1 sp, ch 1) twice. Join as before.

Rnd 4: Sl st in next 2 dc and in next corner sp; starting corner group in same sp; * ch 1, (2dc in next ch-1 sp, ch 1) 3 times; corner group in next corner sp. Rep from * around, end with ch 1. Join. Fasten off.

Rnd 5: Attach Black to any corner sp, starting corner group in same sp; * ch 1, ** 2 dc in next ch-1 sp, ch 1. Rep from ** to next corner sp; corner group in next corner sp. Rep from * around, end with ch 1. Join. Fasten off.

Rnd 6: Attach Burnt Orange to any corner sp, then work as for Rnd 5. Do not fasten off.

Rnd 7: Ch 3, dc in next 2 dc; * in next corner sp make 2 dc, ch 1 and 2 dc; dc in next 3 dc, dc in next ch-1 sp, (dc in next 2 dc, dc in next sp) 5 times; dc in next 3 dc. Rep from * around, end with ch 1. Join— motif completed. Fasten off. Attach Orange to next corner sp.

Now work Strip Section along one side of motif as follows:

Row 1: Ch 3, dc in next dc and in each dc across to next corner ch-1 sp, dc in corner sp—28 dc, counting ch-3 as 1 dc. Ch 3, turn.

Row 2: Dc in next 26 dc, dc in top of ch-3. Fasten off Orange, attach Black. Ch 3, turn.

Rows 3—7: Rep Row 2 for st patt, work:

  2 rows Black
  2 rows Orange
  1 row Burnt Orange.

Ch 3, turn.

Row 8: Dc in next 2 dc, * ch 1, sk 1 dc, dc in next 2 dc. Rep from * to ch-3, dc in top of ch-3. Fasten off, attach Black. Ch 3, turn.

Row 9: Dc in next dc, ch 1, 2 dc in next ch-1 sp, ch 1, * sk 2 dc, 2 dc in next ch-1 sp, ch 1. Rep from * to last 2 dc and turning chain, sk next dc, dc in next dc, dc in top of ch-3. Fasten off, attach Yellow. Ch 3, turn.

Row 10: Make 2 dc in first ch-1 sp, * ch 1, 2 dc in next ch-1 sp. Rep from * to last dc and turning chain, sk next dc, dc in top of ch-3. Fasten off.

† Motif B with Stripe Section: Work as for Motif A and Stripe Section until Row 6 is completed. Do not break off Burnt Orange; ch 1, turn.

Joining of 2 Pieces: With blue markers facing each other, place edge of Row 6 just completed in back of the center free edge of previous motif, then working through both thicknesses, sc in each st across. Fasten off †. Rep directions from † to † 4 more times.

Pin panels to measurements, dampen and leave to dry.

With green, mark Row 10 at narrow edge of 3 panels for top edge; with green, mark the center free edge of end motif of remaining 3 panels. Then with blue markers facing each other and having all green markers at same end, using Burnt Orange and alternating panels, sc the panels together. Remove all markers.

EDGING

With joining rows facing, attach Burnt Orange to corner following a narrow edge, ch 3; keeping work flat dc evenly across the long edge to next corner. Fasten off. Work Edging along other long edge in same way, having the same number of sts. With joining rows facing, attach Black to corner at beg of a narrow edge, ch 3, dc evenly across narrow edge to next corner. Fasten off. Work Edging along opposite edge in same way.

FRINGE

Cut 6 strands of Black, each 18″ long. Double these strands to form a loop. With joining rows facing, insert hook from back to front in first st of one narrow edge and draw loop through. Draw ends through loop and pull tightly to form a knot. Knot 6 strands as before in every 3rd st across. Work fringe along opposite edge. Trim fringe.

Square at a Time

Size
51″ × 68″

Materials
Coats & Clark Red Heart Tweedy 4 Ply Handknitting Yarn:
21 oz Blush Indigo
Coats & Clark Red Heart 4 ply handknitting yarn:
14 oz Claret
21 oz Robin Blue
Size 10, straight knitting needles *(or size required for gauge)*

Gauge
11 sts = 3″
7 rows = 1″
Each Quarter of a Square measures 8½″

Note
Each Square of Afghan consists of 4 quarters.

Instructions
SQUARE A QUARTER (make 4)
With Indigo, cast on 60 sts. This cast-on row will become part of outer edge of the Square.

Row 1: Knit. Mark Row 1 for right side.

Row 2: K28, K2 tog, place a marker, K2 tog, K28. Break off Indigo, attach Claret.

Row 3: Knit.

Row 4: K to 2 sts before marker, K2 tog, sl marker, K2 tog, K remaining sts. Always sl marker on every row.

Repeating Rows 3 and 4 alternately, work:
14 more rows with Claret,

8 rows Indigo,
8 rows Blue,
then continuing with Indigo work until 4 sts remain on needle.

Next Row: Removing marker, K4.

Following Row: (K2 tog) twice.

Last Row: K2 tog. Fasten off. This corner will be at center of the Square.

Leaving the 2 outer edges formed by cast-on sts free, sew the 4 quarters together matching colors, to form Square A. Make 5 more of Square A.

SQUARE B QUARTER (make 4)
With Indigo, cast on 60 sts. Work same as for Quarter of Square A, using colors as follows:

2 rows Indigo,
16 rows Blue,
8 rows Indigo,
8 rows Claret;

work remaining rows with Indigo.

Sew quarters together in same way as for Square A.

Make 5 more of Square B.

Alternating Squares A and B, sew 3 by 4 squares together to form the afghan. With right-side facing, using Indigo and being careful to keep work flat, work a row of sc around the entire outer edge of afghan, making 3 sc in each corner. Fasten off.

FRINGE
Cut 6 strands of Blue, each 18″ long. Double these strands to form a loop. Insert hook from back to front at corner of one narrow edge and draw loop through. Draw loose ends through loop, pull tightly to form knot. Knot 6 strands as before, 60 times in all evenly spaced along narrow edge. Work fringe along other narrow edge in same way. Trim fringe.

[CROCHETED]
Pretty Patchwork

Size
50" × 61"

Materials
Coats & Clark Red Heart 4 ply handknitting yarn:
    14 oz Wood Brown (#360)
    14 oz Lt. Olive (#651)
    10½ oz Bisque (#331)
    10½ oz Bright Pink (#741)
Size K Crochet Hook (*or size required for gauge*)

Gauge
11 dc = 4"
4 rows = 2¼"

Instructions
Rectangle No. 1: With Pink, ch 32.

    Row 1 (right side): Dc in 4th ch from hook and in each ch across—30 dc, counting ch-3 as 1 dc. With a different color yarn mark this row for right side of afghan; ch 3, turn.

Row 2: Dc in next dc and in each dc across, dc in top of ch-3; ch 3, turn.

Repeating Row 2 for pattern, work 13 more rows. Fasten off Pink, attach Bisque; ch 3, turn.

Rectangle No. 2: With Bisque, work 15 rows to make No. 2 shown on Chart. Fasten off.

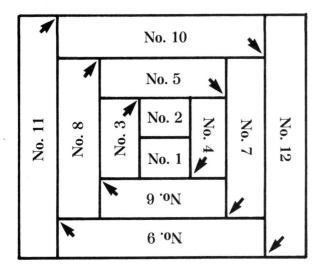

Rectangle No. 3: Attach Olive to corner marked with arrow on No. 3 on Chart.

Row 1: Working in end st of each row, ch 3, make 45 dc evenly spaced across side edge of last 2 rectangles, making the last dc in next corner: 46 dc, counting ch-3 as 1 dc; ch 3, turn. Now work even as for Row 2 of Rectangle No. 1 until 15 rows in all have been worked for this rectangle. Fasten off.

Rectangle No. 4: Attach Brown to marked corner on No. 4 on Chart and work as for No. 3.

Rectangle No. 5: Attach Pink to marked corner on No. 5 on Chart.

Row 1: Ch 3, make 22 dc along edge of No. 4, dc in the 30 dc of No. 2, 23 dc along edge of No.

3 to next corner—76 sts; ch 3, turn. Work even until 15 rows in all have been worked for this rectangle. Fasten off.

Rectangle No. 6: Attach Bisque to marked corner on No. 6 on Chart and work to correspond with No. 5.

Rectangle No. 7: Attach Olive to marked corner on No. 7 on Chart.

Row 1: Ch 3, make 22 dc along edge of No. 6, dc in the 46 dc on No. 4, 23 dc along edge of No. 5: 92 sts. Ch 3, turn. Work 14 more rows. Fasten off.

Rectangle No. 8: Attach Brown to marked corner on No. 8 on Chart and work to correspond with No. 7.

Rectangle No. 9: Attach Pink to marked corner on No. 9 on Chart.

Row 1: Ch 3, 22 dc along edge of No. 8, dc in the 76 dc of No. 6, 23 dc along edge of No. 7: 122 sts; ch 3, turn. Work 14 more rows. Fasten off.

Rectangle No. 10: Attach Bisque to marked corner on No. 10 on Chart and work to correspond with No. 9.

Rectangle No. 11: Attach Olive to marked corner on No. 11 on Chart.

Row 1: Ch 3, 22 dc along edge of No. 10, dc in the 92 dc of No. 8, 23 dc along edge of No. 9: 138 sts; ch 3, turn. Work 14 more rows. Fasten off.

Rectangle No. 12: Attach Brown to marked corner on No. 12 on Chart and complete to correspond with No. 11.

Pin to measurements, dampen and leave to dry.

FRINGE

Cut 6 strands of Olive, each 20″ long. Double these strands to form a loop, insert hook from back to front at corner of Brown narrow edge and draw loop through. Draw loose ends through loop and pull tightly to form knot. Knot 6 strands as before in every 3rd st across narrow edge. Using Brown, work fringe along Olive narrow edge in same way. Trim fringe.

[KNITTED]

San Diego Sunset

designed by Rita Weiss

One of the nice things about living on the west coast is seeing the beautiful sunsets over the Pacific. The magnificent colors of a summer sunset are repeated in this afghan, which is just the perfect weight for a cool summer evening at the ocean. The afghan is made with two colors of worsted weight yarn and an accent of mohair yarn. If you prefer, the entire afghan can be made with three colors of worsted weight.

Size

40″ × 60″ before fringing

Materials

Worsted weight yarn:
    18 oz orange
    5 oz gold
Mohair yarn:
    9 oz fuchsia
Size 15, 36″ circular knitting needle (*or size required for gauge*)

Gauge

In stock st, 5 sts = 2″

Note

Circular needle is used to accommodate large number of stitches. Do not join; work back and forth in rows.

Instructions

With fuchsia, cast on 106 sts loosely.

Row 1 (right side): Purl.

Row 2: Knit.

Row 3: Purl. Finish off fuchsia; join orange.

Row 4: P2; * P2 tog, P13, P2 tog; rep from * across to last 2 sts, P2: 94 sts.

Row 5: K2; * sl 1 as if to knit, K1, PSSO, K11, K2 tog; rep from * across to last 2 sts, K2: 82 sts.

Row 6: Knit.

Row 7: K5; * (YO twice, K1) 7 times, YO twice, K6; rep from * across, ending last rep with K5 instead of K6.

Row 8: K5; * (Knit first YO, drop next YO, K1) 7 times; knit first YO, drop next YO, K6; rep from * across, ending last rep with K5 instead of K6: 130 sts.

Row 9: K2; * sl 1 as if to knit, K1, PSSO, K17, K2 tog; rep from * across to last 2 sts, K2; 118 sts. Finish off orange; join fuchsia.

Row 10: P2; * P2 tog, P15, P2 tog; rep from * to last 2 sts, P2: 106 sts.

Rows 11—19: Rep rows 1 through 9. Finish off orange; join gold.

Row 20: Rep row 10.

Row 21: Purl.

Row 22: P4, knit to last 4 sts, P4.

Row 23: Purl.

Row 24: Rep row 22.

Row 25: Purl. Finish off gold; join orange.

Rows 26—32: Rep rows 4 through 10.

Rep rows 1 through 32 six times more.

Rep rows 1 through 10 once.

Rep rows 1 and 2.

FRINGE

Follow Basic Fringe Instructions on page 16 and make Spaghetti Fringe. Cut 14″ long strands of fuchsia. Knot one strand in each stitch across both short ends of afghan.

[KNITTED]

Golden Sunshine

designed by Rita Weiss

When there's snow on the ground, just wrap yourself in this afghan. You'll surely dream of golden sunshine.

Size

40″ × 60″ before fringing

Materials

Worsted weight yarn:
    22 oz yellow
Size 15, 36″ circular knitting needle *(or size required for gauge)*

Notes

1. A circular needle is used to accommodate large number of stitches. Do not join; work back and forth in rows.

2. To make a YO before a purl stitch, bring yarn around right needle from front to back, then back around into position for purling; purl next stitch.

Gauge

In patt, 17 sts (one patt rep) = 5″

Instructions

Cast on 129 sts. Knit 9 rows. Then work in patt as follows:

Row 1: K5; * (P2 tog) 3 times; (YO, K1) 5 times; YO; (P2 tog) 3 times; rep from * to last 5 sts, K5.

Row 2: K5, P119, K5.

Row 3: Knit.

Row 4: K5, P119, K5.

Rep rows 1 through 4 until piece measures approx 58″ ending with row 1 of patt.

Knit 9 rows and bind off loosely.

FRINGE

Follow Single Knot Fringe Instructions on page 16. Cut strands 16″ long; use 8 strands in each knot. Tie knots evenly spaced across short ends of afghan.

120

Desert Stripes
designed by Barbara Hunter

The muted earth tones of the desert are reflected in this heavy afghan worked in a Star Stitch.

Size
42″ × 54″ before fringing

Materials
Worsted weight yarn:
    28 oz Burnt Orange
    24 oz Gold
    16 oz Honey Beige
Size M wood crochet hook *(or size required for gauge)*

Gauge
In Star Stitch, measured from eye to eye,
one st = 1″
one pattern row (2 rows of crochet) = 1¼″

> ### Notes
> **1.** Afghan is worked with 2 strands of yarn throughout.
>
> **2.** To change color at end of sc row: draw up a loop in last st (2 loops on hook); change to new color, YO, draw through rem 2 lps; ch 3, turn.

Instructions
With Color A, ch 98 loosely.

STAR STITCH PATTERN

Row 1: Draw up a loop in 2nd ch from hook; bringing each loop to the level of the first loop, draw up a loop in next 3 ch (5 loops on hook); YO and draw through all loops on hook; ch 1 to form "eye" of star: 1 Star St made. * Draw up a loop in the eye, draw up a loop in the BACK loop of the last loop drawn up on previous row, and in next 2 ch on previous chain (5 loops on hook); YO and draw through all 5 loops on hook; ch 1 for eye. Rep from * across; sc in 1st ch; ch 1, turn. (47 Star St patterns).

Row 2: Sc in eye, * 2 sc in next eye; Rep from * across to last eye, sc in eye, sc in top of turning ch; ch 3, turn.

Row 3: Draw up a loop in 2nd and 3rd chs from hook (3 loops on hook); sk the first sc, draw up a loop in the BACK loop in the next 2 sc: (5 loops on hook); YO and draw through all loops on hook; ch 1 for eye, * draw up a loop in the eye, draw up a loop in the BACK loop of the last loop drawn up on previous Star St; then in the BACK loop of the next 2 sc (5 loops on hook); YO and draw through all loops on hook, ch 1 for eye. Rep from * across to last sc, sc in last sc; ch 1, turn.

> ### Note
> Rows 3 & 2 = 1 Pattern Row and are repeated throughout.

Work 6 Pattern Rows in Color A, ending with Row 2.

Attach Color B to last stitch. Fasten off A; ch 3, turn.

DC PATTERN

Row 1: Dc in next dc and in each dc across. Ch 3, turn.

Row 2: Rep Row 1.

Row 3: Rep Row 1 ending by attaching Color C to last st. Fasten off Color B.

Work Rows 3 and 2 in Star Stitch pattern for 6 pattern rows. Attach Color B on last st of last pattern row. Fasten off Color C. Work 3 rows of DC pattern attaching Color A on last st of Row 2 of last pattern row. Fasten off Color B.

Color sequence is as follows:

    *6 Pattern Rows Color A
    3 dc rows in Color B
    6 Pattern Rows Color C
    3 dc rows in Color B

Rep from * 1 more time.

Rep 6 Pattern Rows of Color A ending with Row 2. Finish off, weave in all loose ends.

FRINGE

Follow Single Knot Fringe Instructions on page 16. Cut Honey Beige strands 16″ long and use 4 strands in each knot. Tie knot in the bottom stitch of each eye pattern across each short end of afghan.

[KNITTED]

Fire and Flames

designed by Rita Weiss

What can be nicer on a cold winter's evening than to curl up in front of a roaring fire? If your house doesn't have a fireplace, just cover yourself with this afghan; its bright colors will almost make you believe that a roaring fire is at hand.

Size

40″ × 61½″ before fringing

Materials

Bulky weight yarn:
  14 oz Bright Raspberry *(Color A)*
  6 oz Bright Red *(Color B)*
  6 oz Orange *(Color C)*
  6 oz Yellow *(Color D)*
  6 oz Coral *(Color E)*
Size 13, 36″ circular knitting needle *(or size required for gauge)*

Gauge

In patt stitch, 8 sts = 3″

Note

Circular needle is used to accommodate large number of stitches; do not join; work back and forth in rows.

Instructions

With Color A, cast on 105 sts. Knit 6 rows for garter st border.

PATTERN STITCH

Row 1: K4 (for garter st border); purl to last 4 sts, K4 (garter st border).

Row 2 (right side): Knit.

Row 3: K4; P3, * wrap yarn around needle two times, P4, rep from * across to last 6 sts; wrap yarn around needle two times, P2, K4. Finish off Color A; join Color B.

Row 4: K6, drop both wraps; with yarn at back of work, sl 1 as if to purl; * K1, insert right-hand needle

into next st two rows below (**Fig 1**), wrap yarn around needle as if to knit and pull this loop through loosely; knit next st, then pass loop over this knit st; K1, drop both wraps; with yarn at **back** of work, sl 1 as if to purl, rep from * to last 6 sts, K6.

Row 5: K4, P2; with yarn at front of work, sl 1 as if to purl, * P3; with yarn at **front** of work, sl 1 as if to purl; rep from * to last 6 sts; P2, K4.

Row 6: Knit.

Row 7: K4, P3 * wrap yarn around needle two times, P4; rep from * to last 6 sts; wrap yarn around needle two times, P2, K4.

Rep rows 4–7 in following color sequence:

  *4 rows Color C
  4 rows Color D
  4 rows Color E
  4 rows Color A
  4 rows Color B

Rep from * 9 times more; then work as follows:

  *4 rows Color C
  4 rows Color D
  4 rows Color E
  3 rows Color A

Next Row: With Color A, K4, purl to last 4 sts, K4.

Knit 6 more rows with Color A. Bind off loosely in knit.

Weave in all ends. Lightly steam edges.

FRINGE

Follow Triple Knot Fringe Instructions on page 16. Cut strands 22″ long and use 4 strands in each knot. Tie knot through every other cast-on or bound-off stitch across each short end of afghan.

[KNITTED]
Fisherman Ripple

The beauty of off-white fisherman yarn, combined with an interesting textured stitch, makes a lovely cover-up.

Size

46″ × 54″ before fringing

Materials

Dawn Sayelle knitting worsted weight yarn:
    36 oz Fisherman
Size 10½, 36″ circular knitting needle (or size required for gauge)

Gauge

In garter st (knit each row), 7 sts = 2″

Instructions

Note
Throughout patt, each YO counts as one st.

Cast on 187 sts loosely. Do not join; work back and forth in rows. Knit first 2 rows; then work in pattern stitch as follows.

Rows 1, 3, 5, 7 and 9 (right side): K3, * YO, K3; sl 1 as to knit, K1, PSSO; YO, sl 1 as to knit, K2 tog, PSSO; YO, K2 tog; K3, YO, K1; rep from * to last 2 sts, K2.

Rows 2, 4, 6 and 8: K2 (for garter st edge); purl to last 2 sts, K2 (for garter st edge).

Row 10 (wrong side): Knit.

Row 11: K2, purl to last 2 sts, K2.

Row 12: Knit.

Rep Rows 1 through 12 until afghan measures approx 54″ long, ending by working Row 10. Knit one more row, then bind off all sts loosely in knit. Weave in all ends. Lightly steam press on wrong side.

FRINGE

Follow Single Knot Fringe Instructions on page 16. Fringe each short end of afghan. Cut 18″ strands of yarn, use 10 strands for each knot. Tie one knot at each upper and lower point.

[CROCHETED]

Dusty Rose Shells

designed by Eleanor Denner

Easy shells to make a heavy, very warm afghan when worked with two strands of yarn on a K hook. This is a perfect afghan for the coldest winter night.

Size

38″ × 56″ before fringing

Materials

Worsted weight yarn:
    54 oz Dusty Rose
Size K aluminum crochet hook *(or size required for gauge)*

Gauge

In patt with two strands of yarn, 6 shells = 5″

Note
Afghan is worked with two strands of yarn held together throughout.

Instructions

Ch 138 loosely.

Row 1: Sc in 2nd ch from hook and in each ch across: 137 sc; ch 3, turn.

Row 2: Sk 2 sc, work a shell of (dc, ch 1, dc) all in next sc; * sk 2 sc, shell of (dc, ch 1, dc) all in next sc; rep from * across to last 2 sts, sk 1 sc, dc in last sc; ch 1, turn.

Row 3: Sc in first sc; work (sc, ch 1, sc) in each ch-1 sp across row to last st, sc in top of turning ch, ch 3, turn.

Rep Rows 2 and 3 for pattern until afghan measures 56″ long, ending by working Row 2.

Last Row: Sc in each dc and ch-1 sp across. Finish off.

FRINGE

Work Double Knot Fringe (see page 16) across each short end of afghan. Cut strands 20″ long, and use 8 strands in each knot. Space knots with 2 sts in between.

126

CHAPTER 6

BABY

Weekends

It takes 9 months to make a baby—but only a weekend to make a beautiful afghan to welcome it. These afghans aren't just for babies—toddlers, too love to have their own pretty cover-ups. And, made in appropriate colors, each baby afghan in this chapter can be a pretty Lapghan for an adult.

[KNITTED]

Sweet Sherbet

designed by Barbara Hunter

Baby is sure to thank you with joyful coos as she or he drifts off to dreamland under this cozy afghan.

Size

33″ × 35″

Materials

Worsted weight mohair-type yarn:
   11 oz pastel ombre
14″ long size 11 straight needles *(or size required for gauge)*
Two stitch markers

Gauge

In garter st (K each row) 3 sts = 1″

Instructions

Cast on 116 sts and knit 10 rows for garter st border.

Then work in patt as follows.

PATTERN STITCH

Row 1: K7, place marker for end of side border, purl to last 7 sts, place marker for beg of side border, K7.

Row 2: K7, slip marker, K1; * YO, K3, pass the first of the 3 knit sts over the 2nd and 3rd sts; rep from * to last 2 sts before marker, K2, slip marker, K7.

Row 3: K7, purl to marker, slip marker, K7.

Row 4: K7, slip marker, K2; * YO, K3, pass the first of the 3 knit sts over the 2nd and 3rd sts; rep from * to last st before marker, K1, slip marker, K7.

Row 5: K7, purl to marker, K7.

Rows 6 through 10: Knit.

Rep these 10 rows 14 more times, ending with row 5 on last rep.

Knit 10 rows.

Bind off.

[KNITTED]

Buttercup

Fresh as a field of spring flowers, this square afghan will wrap baby in lightweight warmth.

Size

36″ square before fringing

Materials

Dawn Wintuk pompadour baby weight yarn:
    14 oz Buttercup
Size 6, 29″ circular knitting needle (or size required for gauge)

Gauge

In garter st (knit each row), 11 sts = 2″

Instructions

Cast on 199 sts loosely. Do not join; work back and forth in rows. Knit first 5 rows for garter st border. Then work in pattern stitch as follows.

Row 1 (right side): K3, K2 tog; * YO, K3, YO; sl 1, K2 tog, PSSO; rep from * to last 8 sts; YO, K3, YO; sl 1, K1, PSSO; K3.

Row 2: K5; * P3, K3; rep from * to last 8 sts; P3, K5.

Row 3: K3, P2; * K3, P3; rep from * to last 8 sts; K3, P2, K3.

Row 4: Rep Row 2.

Row 5: K5; * YO, sl 1, K2 tog. PSSO; YO, K3; rep from * to last 8 sts; YO, sl 1, K2 tog, PSSO; YO, K5.

Row 6: K3, P2; * K3, P3; rep from * to last 8 sts; K3, P2, K3.

Row 7: K5; * P3, K3; rep from * to last 8 sts; P3, K5.

Row 8: Rep Row 6.

Rep Rows 1 through 8 until afghan measures approx 35″ from cast-on edge, ending by working Row 5. Knit 4 more rows for garter st border. Bind off all sts loosely in knit. Finish off; weave in all ends.

FRINGE

Following Single Knot Fringe instructions on page 16, fringe cast-on and bound-off edges. Cut 10″ strands of yarn, use 3 strands for each knot; tie knots evenly spaced across, about every 3rd st.

Wee Bonnie Plaid

Here's a soft and lovely afghan for a wee baby that's especially fun to make. First you crochet the foundation, then weave in contrasting colors.

Size

36″ × 42″ before fringing

Materials

Dawn Wintuk pompadour baby weight yarn:
    10 oz White
    6 oz Baby Blue
    6 oz Baby Pink
Size D aluminum crochet hook (or size required for gauge)
Tapestry or yarn needle (for weaving)

Gauge

In mesh pattern, (dc, ch 1) 3 times = 1″; 3 rows = 1″

Instructions

MESH BACKGROUND

> **Note**
> Throughout patt, beg ch-4 of each row counts as one dc plus one ch.

With Baby Blue, ch 215 loosely.

Row 1 (foundation row): Dc in 5th ch from hook; * ch 1, sk one ch, dc in next ch; rep from * across = 106 ch-1 sps.

Row 2 (patt row): Ch 4, turn; dc in next dc, * ch 1, sk ch-1 sp, dc in next dc; rep from * across, ending last rep by working dc in 3rd ch of ch-4. Change to Baby Pink. [to change colors: With old color, work last dc of row until 2 lps rem on hook; finish off old color, leaving approx 4″ end for weaving in later. With new color (leave approx 4″ end), complete st (YO and draw through 2 lps on hook) = color changed.]

Rep Row 2 in the following color sequence: * 2 rows Baby Pink, 4 rows White and 2 rows Baby Blue (8 rows total); rep from * 14 times more. You should now have a total of 15 repeats of 8-row color sequence. Finish off; weave in all ends.

WEAVING

> **Note**
> Weaving is worked on mesh background from bottom to top lengthwise, crossing horizontal stripes of color.

Starting at lower right-hand corner, cut three 69″ strands of Baby Blue; thread into tapestry or yarn needle. Leaving 10″ ends for fringing later, insert needle down through first space, then up through next space; continue to weave down and up through first row of sps to top of afghan. At top edge, leave 10″ ends for fringing later. (Be careful not to pull woven strands too tight; keep mesh background flat without puckers.)

Work next row with Baby Blue in same manner; begin by inserting needle up through first sp, then down through next sp, etc.

Continuing to weave in this manner, work remaining rows in the following color sequence: * 2 rows Baby Pink, 4 rows White and 2 rows Baby blue (8 rows total); rep from * until background mesh is completely filled.

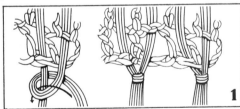

FRINGE

Tie matching pair of strands tog along each short end of afghan as shown in **Fig 1**. Trim fringe evenly to 5″ length.

[KNITTED]
Baby Cables

Cables alternate with stripes of stockinette stitch in this afghan, which would also be pretty worked in a solid color.

Size

36″ square

Materials

Dawn Wintuk baby weight yarn:
    20 oz Lullaby
Size 9, 29″ circular knitting needle *(or size required for gauge)*
Cable needle

Note

Yarn is used doubled throughout afghan.

CABLE PATTERN STITCH

(worked over 8 sts)
Row 1 (right side): P1, K6, P1.
Row 2: K1, P6, K1.
Row 3 (cable twist row): P1, sl next 3 sts onto cable needle and hold at back of work; K3, then K3 from cable needle; P1.
Row 4: Rep Row 2.
Row 5: Rep Row 1.
Row 6: Rep Row 2.
Rep Rows 1 through 6 for patt.

Gauge

With 2 strands of yarn in garter st, 9 sts = 2″

Instructions

With circular needle and 2 strands of yarn (now and throughout afghan), cast on 162 sts loosely. Do not join; work back and forth in rows. Knit first 5 rows for garter st border. INC ROW: K9; * knit in front and back of next st (inc made), K1; inc in next st, K7; rep from * to last 3 sts, K3 = 192 sts. Now work in Cable Patt St as follows.

Row 1 (right side): K8; * P1, K6, P1, K4; rep from * to last 4 sts, K4.

Row 2: K4, P4; * K1, P6, K1, P4; rep from * to last 4 sts, K4.

Row 3: Rep Row 1.

Row 4: Rep Row 2.

Row 5 (cable twist row): K8; * P1, sl next 3 sts onto cable needle and hold at back of work; K3, then K3 from cable needle; P1, K4; rep from * to last 4 sts, K4.

Row 6: Rep Row 2.

Rep Rows 1 through 6 until afghan measures approx 35″ from cast-on edge, ending by working Row 1. DEC ROW: K9; * K2 tog, K1; K2 tog, K7; rep from * to last 3 sts, K3 = 162 sts. Knit 5 more rows for garter st border. Bind off all sts loosely in knit. Weave in all ends.

[KNITTED]
Scarlet Ribbons

This two-color pattern looks like ribbons interwoven—but it's all accomplished with yarn and knitting needles!

Size

34″ × 40″ before fringing

Materials

Dawn Wintuk sport weight yarn:
    9 oz White
    8 oz Flame
Size 9, 29″ circular knitting needle *(or size required for gauge)*

Gauge

In stock st, 5 sts = 1″

Instructions

With White, cast on 172 sts. Do not join; work back and forth in rows.

Row 1 (right side): With White, knit.

Row 2: Continuing with White, knit across. Drop White *(do not cut)*; continue with Flame. *(Color not in use is carried loosely up side of work.)*

Row 3: With Flame, K1, * YB (yarn to back of work), sl 2 (always slip each st as to purl), K2; rep from * to last 3 sts; YB, sl 2, K1.

Row 4: Continuing with Flame, P1, * YF (yarn to front of work), sl 2, P2; rep from * to last 3 sts: YF, sl 2, P1. Drop Flame *(do not cut)*; continue with White.

Rows 5 through 8: Rep Rows 1 through 4. At end of Row 8, continue with Flame *(do not drop)*; drop white.

Row 9: With Flame, knit.

Row 10: Continuing with Flame, knit across. Drop Flame; continue with White.

Row 11: With White, K1, * YB, sl 2, K2; rep from * to last 3 sts; YB, sl 2, K1.

Row 12: Continuing with white, P1, * YF, sl 2, P2; rep from * to last 3 sts; YF, sl 2, P1. Drop White; continue with Flame.

Rows 13 through 16: Rep Rows 9 through 12. At end of Row 16, continue with White *(do not drop)*; drop Flame.

Rep Rows 1 through 16 until afghan measures approx 40″ long, ending by working Row 8. Finish off Flame; continue with White only and knit one more row. Bind off all sts in knit. Weave in all ends.

FRINGE

Following Single Knot Fringe instructions on page 16, cut 14″ strands of White. Use 4 strands for each knot; tie 43 knots across each short end of afghan, having one knot at each White raised vertical stripe.

[CROCHETED]
Shell Stitch

Shells shape a lacy afghan in this pattern. A shell border, worked after the afghan is completed, adds the finishing touch.

Size

30″ × 38″

Materials

Dawn Wintuk pompadour baby weight yarn:
  14 oz Buttercup
Size E aluminum crochet hook (*or size required for gauge*)

Gauge

In dc, 11 sts = 2″

Instructions

Ch 159 loosely.

Row 1: Dc in 4th ch from hook and in each rem ch across = 157 dc (counting beg ch-3).

Note
Ch-3 counts as one dc throughout patt.

Row 2: Ch 3, turn; dc in next dc and in each rem dc across, ending by working last dc in top of ch-3.

Rows 3 and 4: Rep Row 2, twice.

Row 5 (foundation shell row): Ch 3, turn; dc in each of next 6 dc; * † sk 2 dc, work (dc, ch 1, dc, ch 1, dc, ch 1, dc) all in next dc (shell made); sk 2 dc, dc in next dc †; rep from † to † 3 times; dc in each of next 6 dc; rep from * across.

Row 6 (shell patt row): Ch 3, turn; dc in each of next 6 dc; * † work a shell in center sp of next shell, dc in dc between shells †; rep from † to † twice; work a shell in center sp of next shell, dc in each of next 7 dc; rep from * across.

Rows 7 through 12: Rep Row 6, six times. You should now have 8 shell rows.

Row 13: Ch 3, turn; dc in each of next 6 dc; * † ch 2, sc in center sp of next shell; ch 2, dc in dc between shells †; rep from † to † twice; ch 2, sc in center sp of next shell; ch 2, dc in each of next 7 dc; rep from * across.

Row 14: Ch 3, turn; dc in each of next 6 dc; * † 2 dc in ch-2 sp, dc in sc; 2 dc in next ch-2 sp, dc in dc †; rep from † to † 3 times; dc in each of next 6 dc; rep from * across = 157 dc.

Row 15: Ch 3, turn; dc in next dc and in each rem dc across.

Rep Rows 5 through 15, 8 times more; then rep Row 15 twice more. Do not finish off; continue with edging as follows.

EDGING

Rnd 1: Ch 4, turn. Working across last row just worked: In first dc, work (dc, ch 1, dc, ch 1, dc) for beg corner shell; sk 2 dc, shell in next dc; * sk 2 dc, dc in next dc; sk 2 dc, shell in next dc; rep from * to within 3 sts from next corner; sk 2 dc, shell in top of ch-3 (corner shell). Working across side edge along end of rows: Sk first row, shell in next row; * sk one row, dc in next row, shell in next row; rep from * to last row, sk last row. Working across foundation chain edge: Shell in first st (corner shell), sk 2 dc, shell in next st; * sk 2 sts, dc in next st; sk 2 sts, shell in next st; rep from * to within 3 sts from next corner; sk 2 sts, shell in last st (corner shell). Working across last edge along end of rows: Sk first row, shell in next row; * sk one row, dc in next row, shell in next row; rep from * to last row, sk last row; join with a sl st in 3rd ch of beg ch-4.

Rnd 2: Do not turn. Sl st in ch-1, sl st in next dc and then into center sp of beg corner shell; ch 4. In same sp, work 5 dc with ch 1 between each dc. * Shell in center sp of next shell; † dc in dc between shells, shell in center sp of next shell †; rep from † to † to next corner shell. In center sp of corner shell, work 6 dc with ch 1 between each dc. Rep from * 3 times more, ending last rep without working corner shell. Join with a sl st in 3rd ch of beg ch-4. Finish off; weave in all ends.

Mint Flip

This is a good afghan for a beginning knitter. The pattern is easy but the look is great!

Size

40″ square

Materials

Dawn Sayelle knitting worsted weight yarn:
    18 oz Baby Green
Size 11, 29″ circular knitting needle *(or size required for gauge)*

Gauge

In garter stitch (knit each row), 3 sts = 1″

Instructions

Cast on 122 sts loosely. Do not join; work back and forth in rows. Knit first 6 rows for garter stitch border. Then work in pattern stitch as follows.

Row 1: K10, * P3, K6; rep from * to last 4 sts, K4.

Row 2: K4 (garter stitch edge), P6; * K3, P6; rep from * to last 4 sts, K4 (garter stitch edge).

Row 3: Rep Row 1.

Row 4: Rep Row 2.

Row 5: Rep Row 1.

Row 6: Rep Row 2.

Row 7: Rep Row 1.

Row 8: Rep Row 2.

Row 9 (patt reverse row): Rep Row 2.

Row 10: Rep Row 1.

Row 11: Rep Row 2.

Row 12: Rep Row 1.

Rep Rows 1 through 12 until afghan measures approx 39″ long, ending by working Row 7. Knit 6 more rows for garter stitch border. Bind off all sts loosely in knit. Weave in all ends.

Cuddly Kittens

This pretty pattern looks just like rows of kittens. It's easy and quick to make.

Size

38″ by 44″ before fringing

Materials

Dawn Sayelle knitting worsted weight yarn:
    16 oz White
    12 oz Baby Blue
    8 oz True Blue
Size H aluminum crochet hook *(or size required for gauge)*

Gauge

5 Shells = 7″
Gauge Note: Each shell = (2 dc, ch 1, 2 dc).

Instructions

With Baby Blue, ch 139 loosely.

Row 1 (right side): Dc in 4th ch from hook; dc in next ch, sk 2 chs, work beg shell over next 2 chs as follows: 2 dc in next ch, ch 1, 2 dc in next ch (beg shell made). * Sk 3 chs, work beg shell over next 2 chs (as before); rep from * to last 5 chs; sk 2 chs, dc in each of last 3 chs = 26 shells.

Row 2: Ch 3, turn; dc in each of next 2 dc, * work (2 dc, ch 1, 2 dc) in ch-1 sp of next shell (shell made); rep from * to last 2 dc, dc in each of last 2 dc; dc in top of ch-3, changing to White. [To Change Colors: Work dc until 2 lps rem on hook; finish off color being used, leaving approx 4″ end for weaving in now or later. With new color (leave approx 4″ end), YO and draw through 2 lps on hook = color changed.]

Row 3: With White, ch 3, turn; dc in each of next 2 dc, work puff st (abbreviated PS) in sp before first shell in 2nd row below as follows: Work (YO and insert hook in sp before first shell in 2nd row below—**Fig 1**; hook yarn and draw up a long lp to height of working row) 4 times (9 lps now on hook—**Fig 2**); YO and draw through first 8 lps on hook, then YO and draw through rem 2 lps on hook = PS made. * Work a shell in ch-1 sp of next shell (in working row), work PS in next sp between shells in 2nd row below; rep from * to last shell; work a shell in ch-1 sp of last shell, work PS in sp after last shell in 2nd row below; dc in each of last 2 dc (in working row), dc in top of ch-3 = 27 PS.

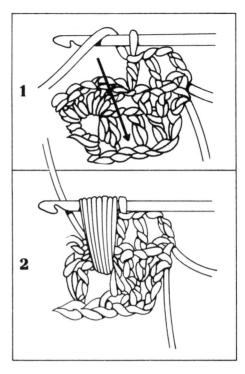

Row 4: Ch 3, turn; dc in each of next 2 dc, * sk PS, work shell in ch-1 sp of next shell; rep from * to last PS; sk last PS, dc in each of last 2 dc, dc in top of ch-3 = 26 shells.

Row 5: Rep Row 2, changing to True Blue in last dc.

Rows 6 and 7: With True blue, rep Rows 3 and 4.

Row 8: With True Blue, rep Row 2, changing to White in last dc.

Rows 9 and 10: With White, rep Rows 3 and 4.

Row 11: With White, rep Row 2, changing to Baby Blue in last dc.

Rows 12 and 13: With Baby Blue, rep Rows 3 and 4.

Row 14: With Baby Blue, rep Row 2, changing to White in last dc.

Rep Rows 3 through 14, 4 times more; then rep Rows 3 through 13 once more. *(You should now have 2 rows of Baby Blue at top edge.)* Finish off; weave in all ends.

FRINGE

Following Single Knot Fringe instructions on page 16, fringe each short end of afghan. Cut 12″ strands of Baby Blue. Use 2 strands for each knot. Tie one knot in every other st across edge.

Peppermint Ripple

An unusual "arrowhead" ripple pattern makes up this sweet pink cover. Its square size is nice for wrapping the tiniest baby.

Size

40″ square

Materials

Dawn Wintuk sport weight yarn:
   11 oz Pink
Size 10, 29″ circular knitting needle (*or size required for gauge*)

Gauge

In seed st, 9 sts = 2″

SEED STITCH PATTERN

(worked on even number of sts)
Row 1: * K1, P1; rep from * across.
Row 2: * P1, K1; rep from * across.
Rep Rows 1 and 2 for patt.

Instructions

Cast on 184 sts loosely. Do not join; work back and forth in rows. Work 5 rows in Seed Stitch Patt, ending by working Row 1. Then work in pattern stitch as follows.

Row 1 (wrong side): (P1, K1) twice (for seed st edge); purl to last 4 sts, (P1, K1) twice (for seed st edge).

Row 2: (K1,P1) twice; knit to last 4 sts, (K1,P1) twice.

Row 3: (P1,K1) twice; * K4, P8, K4; rep from * to last 4 sts, (P1,K1) twice.

Row 4: (K1,P1) twice; *P3, K2 tog; K3, (YO) twice, K3; sl 1 as to knit, K1, PSSO, P3; rep from * to last 4 sts, (K1,P1) twice.

Note

Throughout patt, each YO counts as one st.

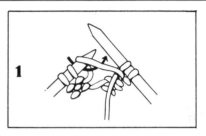

Row 5: (P1,K1) twice; * K3, P4; purl in front of first YO, then purl in back of next YO (**Fig 1**); P4, K3; rep from * to last 4 sts, (P1,K1) twice.

Row 6: (K1,P1) twice; * P2, K2 tog, K3; YO, K2, YO, K3; sl 1 as to knit, K1, PSSO, P2; rep from * to last 4 sts, (K1,P1) twice.

Row 7: (P1,K1) twice; *K2, P12, K2; rep from * to last 4 sts, (P1,K1) twice.

Row 8: (K1,P1) twice; * P1, K2 tog, K3; YO, K4, YO, K3; sl 1 as to knit, K1, PSSO, P1; rep from * to last 4 sts, (K1,P1) twice.

Row 9: (P1,K1) twice; * K1, P14, K1; rep from * to last 4 sts, (P1,K1) twice.

Row 10: (K1,P1) twice; * K2 tog, K3; YO, K6, YO, K3; sl 1 as to knit, K1, PSSO; rep from * to last 4 sts, (K1,P1) twice.

Rep Rows 1 through 10 until afghan measures approx 40″ long, ending by working Row 2. Then work 4 rows in Seed Stitch Patt (beg with Row 2). Bind off all sts in Seed stitch. Weave in all ends. Lightly steam press on wrong side.

INDEX

Bold numbers indicate location of color photo.

For information on how you can have *Better Homes & Gardens*
magazine delivered to your door, write to:
Robert Austin, P.O. Box 4536, Des Moines, IA 50336.